THE FEMININE ENTRAPPED WITHIN A FRUIT

A Jungian Interpretation

Inácio Cunha, PhD
Jungian Analyst

CHIRON PUBLICATIONS • ASHEVILLE, NORTH CAROLINA

www.ChironPublications.com

Interior and cover design by Danijela Mijailovic
Cover image - embroidering made by Lys Angela Vasconcellos
Printed primarily in the United States of America.

ISBN 978-1-68503-017-9 paperback
ISBN 978-1-68503-018-6 hardcover
ISBN 978-1-68503-019-3 electronic
ISBN 978-1-68503-020-9 limited edition paperback

Library of Congress Cataloging-in-Publication Data

Names: Cunha, Inácio, 1962- author.
Title: The feminine entrapped within a fruit : a Jungian interpretation / Inácio Cunha.
Description: Asheville, North Carolina : Chiron Publications, [2022] |
Includes bibliographical references. | Summary: "The main purpose of this book is to investigate the archetypal motif of the feminine entrapped within vegetable species (mainly fruits). Several fairy tales, originated in different regions (America, Europe, Africa, and Eastern countries) were analyzed. This motif deals primarily with the dynamic of suppression and repression of the feminine, as well as its redemption, which may occur in the collective consciousness. Throughout the text, the reader will have the chance to observe how the dynamic of suppression and repression of the feminine, as well as its redemption, may occur not only collectively, but also as a subjective happening within the psyche of both man and woman. The symbolical meaning of each fruit portrayed in the tales, the importance of the water, and the shadowy aspects of both the masculine and feminine principles are taken in to enhance the psychological understanding of human psyche, as far as the play of oppositions is concerned. Dreams of modern man and woman are also analyzed to demonstrate the actuality of the theme"-- Provided by publisher.
Identifiers: LCCN 2022026373 (print) | LCCN 2022026374 (ebook) | ISBN 9781685030186 (hardcover) | ISBN 9781685030179 (paperback) | ISBN 9781685030209 (limited edition paperback) | ISBN 9781685030193 (ebook)
Subjects: LCSH: Fruit--Folklore. | Fruit--Symbolic aspects. | Women--Folklore. | Symbolism in folklore. | Femininity in literature. | Psychoanalysis and fairy tales. | Psychoanalysis and folklore. | Jungian psychology.
Classification: LCC GR790.F78 C86 2022 (print) | LCC GR790.F78 (ebook) | DDC 398.09--dc23/eng/20220719
LC record available at https://lccn.loc.gov/2022026373
LC ebook record available at https://lccn.loc.gov/2022026374

PREFACE

When, as a child, I attended primary school, my schoolteacher told the class a very impressive tale. It was about a girl who had been beguiled by an evil woman who ended up sticking a needle into the damsel's ear, transforming her into a little pigeon. Even more embarrassing was to know it all happened because the Prince left her alone, waiting on him while sitting on the branches of a tree. That was a shocking image for a seven-year boy, but, still, it was a relief to know that, at the end, the girl recovered her original form, the evil human was destroyed, and the Prince married the damsel.

It has been over fifty years since this tale had been hovering in my thoughts. And it was only after having acquired the prospective lens offered by Jungian psychology that I could have a better understanding of the symbolical meaning of this imagery. It indeed expresses the ongoing dismissal of the feminine—a condition that is unconscious to many of us.

By being unconscious, much of the suffering we experience nowadays as human beings can be traced to this problem, since it is this principle what allows life to flow. Whatever the feminine principle may be, what we know, and mostly feel, is that life is totally dependent on it.

Whenever this principle is put aside by both man and woman, either objectively or subjectively, we dry up, become stiff, and un-creative. Every time we say "no" to the feminine principle, we die a little.

So, by going through a set of several tales originating from different parts of the world, it was my intention to offer the reader a possible way to extract some psychological understanding posed by these tales in which the entrapment of the feminine is highlighted. By becoming both aware and conscious of this problem, we may participate in the process of its redemption, which is, indeed, the redemption of us all.

Inácio Cunha, PhD
Belo Horizonte, Brazil

Table of Contents

Special thanks to the Stiftung zur Förderung der Psychologie von C.G. Jung for supporting the publication of this book.

CHAPTER 1

THE ENTRAPMENT WITHIN THE FRUIT

The material presented here is an attempt to understand, psychologically, a motif frequently found in fairytales: the entrapment of the feminine element within vegetation species, primarily fruits. What guides this study are the tenets of Jungian Psychology, which rely on the interpretation of the varied forms of human expression as allegories for the subjective psychic processes.

Because there are a great many versions of tales dealing with this motif around the world, the least that can be said about the theme is that it may conceal an important symbolic expression of psychic life that merits investigation. Indeed, such an entrapment is mainly, but not only, connected to the suppression and/or repression of the feminine element in the collective psyche of a world, tinged by patriarchal colors, still recognizable in the modern times. More recently, however, we have witnessed, not without surprise, that the suppression of this element still continues to exist and has increased mainly among women. This study utilizes several tales, among hundreds of versions, to investigate this motif, ones which unfold differently and offer various solutions to similar content within the narratives. In addition to this, each variant presents peculiarities specific to the level of conscious development, geography, time and all the cultural *terroir* from which a given tale has emerged.

Still, even though consulting several versions of the tale provides extensive material to amplify certain motifs, there is also the risk of wandering endlessly without getting to the essence of a given psychic dynamic. The utilization of many versions can hamper reaching to the core of a given motif because the exploration of several minutiae, inherent to each narrative, pulverizes the discussion. And for the reader, moving back and forth across various tales could end up becoming a tiring and hard to follow task.

The tale upon which the interpretation is primarily based is presented in its entirety at the end of this chapter, while its variants, utilized for comparison, are made available abridged to the reader in the appendix. Therefore, it is suggested that the reader first consults the synopsis of each tale, since he or she then will become familiarized with all the material discussed within the body of the writing.

As it is known, no Jungian interpretation should ever be taken as final. Since the material is "symbolic," that is, based on something which is not a given, an individual is always dependent on his or her own psychic development and inner structure to extract meaning out of the "image." Therefore, it is better that the reader remain aware of the fact that this study is liable to be subjected to continuous scrutiny. Since the material of fairytales emerges from an archetypal basis, its meaning is always renovated every time one delves into it, for such stories are eternal.

The motif of the entrapment of the feminine within fruits, greeneries or other vegetation is quite prevalent in mythic tales, folk stories and legends. This theme, made known worldwide through the fairytale "The Three Oranges," of presumed Persian origin[1], can also be seen across several Mediterranean cultures, including the Iberian Peninsula and other regions of the Near East. In Japan, this motif is found in the medieval tale Uriko-hime (Melon Princess), among other versions.[2] There are even other tales in which, instead of a fruit ready to eat, we find one which needs some culinary preparation, such as it is in the case of Cinderella, who resurges from a pumpkin. In these stories, the feminine that

---

[1] C.S. Kawan, Reflections of International Narrative Research on the example of the tale of the Three Oranges, http://www.folklore.ee/folklore/vol27/kawan.pdf. Last access May 2010.

[2] F. H. Mayer & Y. Kunio, "Yanagita Kunio": Japanese Folk Tales. *Folklore Studies,* Vol. 11, No. 1 (1952), i–97, https://doi.org/10.2307/1177324.

was once entrapped inside the fruit is eventually released and redeemed. There are cases, however, where the amalgamation between a human being and greenery has a different connotation because, instead of being entrapped, he or she is transformed into the vegetable itself. This is the case in an Amerindian version of the origin of the manioc shrub, whose eatable portion is its root, commonly found among various Brazilian tribes[3], or in the accounts of the origin of the guaraná (*Paullinia cupana*), a fruit greatly enjoyed in Brazil, now mostly used to prepare soft drinks.[4] In the former tale, the manioc appeared after a white skinned girl had been buried inside a hut; in the latter, the guarana fruit appeared as the eyes of a divine child who had passed away.

According to Machado[5], this theme in Portugal was first recorded in the sixteenth century CE under the title "The Three Citrons of Love," published by Fernão Soropita. Another Portuguese version, documented by Teófilo Braga and also entitled "The Three Citrons of Love," brings in an important variation at the end of the story regarding the fate of the negative feminine figure[6]. There are indications, however, that this theme appeared earlier in more remote regions such as India where there is, for example, a tale called "Bél Princess," here translated as "The Quince Princess."[7]

The variant "The Three Citrons"[8] (without the word "Love") is the Italian version of "The Three Oranges" written down by Giambattista Basile in the book of folktales known as Il Pentamerone, around the second half of the seventeenth century CE. This book was first published in Naples by Basile, Count of Torrone, who died around 1673 and is believed to have gathered tales mostly in Venice and Crete. Also reported in Italy by Calvino,

---

[3] J.V.C. Magalhaes, *O Selvagem*. Ed Sao Paulo, Vol. 16, 86.

[4] N. Pereira, *Os indios Maues*, 176.

[5] J.B. Machado, Análise Informático-linguística de Três Versões do conto As Três Cidras do Amor http://alfarrabio.di.uminho.pt/vercial/zips/machad17.pdf. Last access May 2010.

[6] C. Pedroso, *Contos Populares Portugueses*, 2001, 47-52.

[7] M. Stokes, *Indian Fairy Tales*.

[8] G. Basile, *Project Gutenberg's Stories from Pentamerone*. Last access Dec. 2009.

is a version of the same theme known as the "Little Shepherd," where the fruit is referred to as an apple.[9] The version of "The Love of The Three Oranges" consulted here was translated into English from the original Italian in 1885.[10]

In Brazil, the first version of this theme was registered in 1885 by Silvio Romero under the title, "The Story of The Crooked Mooress" (A Estória da Moura Torta) and then later by Ruth Guimarães with the title "The Little Dove and The Crooked Mooress" (A Pombinha e a Moura Torta).[11]

Considering the great variability between tales that deal with the same subject, the task to choose one to be analyzed psychologically is rather difficult. Usually, we would primarily look for the oldest version, or the most "complete" one, or maybe the version which has not acquired too many subsequent or modern additions. These criteria increase the chances that such a version will be less adulterated, thus representing a more genuine unconscious process, which is the main object of interest for interpretation.

In this present study however, the version of Sílvio Romero — "The Story of The Crooked Mooress"[12]— is utilized as a conductive thread for the interpretation, even though it is not so rich in details and has fewer elements compared to other versions. This choice was made taking into consideration that it was, possibly, the first version registered in Brazil and was the first I heard as a child. Despite its simplicity, it functions as a frame within which the elements of other versions can be brought in and further analyzed. The complete tale is given below:

---

[9] I. Calvino, *Italian Folktales Selected and Retold*, trans. George Martin http://www.ruanyifeng.com/calvino/2006/10/the_little_shepherd_en.html Last access May 2010.

[10] T.F. Crane, *Italian Popular Tales*, Retrieved from https://www.gutenberg.org/ebooks/23634, November 26, 2007.

[11] R. Guimarães, *Lendas e Fábulas do Brasil*.

[12] S. Romero, *Contos Populares do Brasil*.

THE STORY OF THE CROOKED MOORESS

There was once a father and three sons. Since he had no longer anything to offer to them, he gave each one his sons a watermelon when they decided to leave home and make their own living. Their father instructed them to open the watermelons only when they were close to water.

The eldest son, after deciding to find out what his fate would bring, even though he was still near home, could not refrain from opening his watermelon. A beautiful lady jumped out from inside it, saying "Give me water or give me milk." The young man could find neither one nor the other; and the lady fell back and died.

The middle son, when his turn came, and still not far from home, also opened his watermelon, and from inside came out a more beautiful lady than the first. She asked for water or milk, and the young man found neither of these; so she fell back and died, as well.

When the youngest son went out into the world to seek his living, he was clever and only opened his watermelon when he was near a fountain. As soon as it was open, out jumped a lady who was more beautiful than the first two, saying "I want water or milk." The young man went to the spring, brought her water, and she drank to her content. But the lady was naked, so the young man told her to hide in a nearby tree while he went around to fetch her some clothes. She climbed up and hid amongst the leaves.

Along came a crooked Mooress to get water from the fountain. She saw the image of the beautiful lady in the tree reflected in the water and thought it was her own likeness. She said to herself: "What a cheek! How can such a beautiful lady like me be a water fetcher!" She threw the jug on the ground, breaking it to pieces. When she arrived home, with no water and no jug, she was slapped by her mistress, who told her to go back again for water. But at the fountain the same thing happened, and she broke another jug. Yet a third time, the same scene repeated, but the lady in the tree could not help laughing out loud.

The crooked Mooress, very surprised, looked up and said: "Oh! So it's you, my little granddaughter! ...Let me search for lice in your hair." She climbed swiftly up and, pretending to catch the insects, sank a pin into the lady's head. This turned the lady into a dove, who flew away! The crooked Mooress remained in her place, and when the young man returned with the clothes, he was amazed by the transformation the lady he had left there had undergone. But the usurper Mooress decoyed him: "What do you want? The sun tanned me! You took so long to come back for me!"

They thus left for the palace, where they got married. The dove then remained flying here and there around the palace nearby, and set down in the garden, saying: "Gardener, gardener, how is the king, my master, doing with his crooked Mooress?" Then she flew away. Before long, the gardener told the king about this. So being rather suspicious, the king ordered a diamond noose to be made to catch the dove. However, it was useless, so he had one made of gold, then one of silver, which did not work. At the end, he ordered one made of birdlime in which the dove was trapped. The caged bird was taken to the king, who appreciated it greatly. After a time, the Mooress pretended to be pregnant and made all efforts towards having the bird for a meal. On the day it was to be put into the pan, the king, feeling sorry for it, started to scratch the dove's head. Finding a knob there, and thinking it could be a flea, he picked at the knob and pulled out the pin. A lady, as magnificent as Love, sprang up, and the king recognized his then beautiful princess. They married, and the crooked Mooress was tied to the tails of two savage mules and died after being torn apart.

CHAPTER 2

THE INTERPRETATION

The Characters

The beginning of the story describes an unknown place where there is a father and his three sons. There is no mention of a mother or a daughter at this point. So, already there is the idea that something may not be quite right concerning the balance between the masculine and the feminine principles. In Romero's version, the plotting uses characters whose symbols are closer to consciousness since it refers to a family with ordinary individuals, such as a father and his sons. In other versions, by contrast, the presenting problem strays a little further from consciousness, since the characters encompass elements not seen in everyday life or not common to the human domain. In the version by Ruth Guimarães ("The Little Dove and the Crooked Mooress"), there is no family to begin with but only a prince who sets out to visit his fairy. In the Indian version, "Bél Princess" ("The Quince Princess"), the family is royal and consists of a king, queen, six married princes and one who is reluctant to marry. An Italian version of this tale – "The Three Citrons" – first announces the figure of the king and his son, who is avoiding marriage. Another related Italian tale, collected by Calvino, "The Love of the Three Pomegranates" (L'amore delle tre melagrane),[13] offers a more complete royal

---

[13] Calvino, I. *Fiabe Italiane - raccolte e trascritte da Italo Calvino. Vol. II*. Torino: Einaudi, 449.

family, with a king, a queen and a prince. In this tale, the prince imposes a very specific condition before agreeing to marry: *"Mother, I want to marry a woman as white as milk and as red as blood."* This is the same condition put by the son to the father in "The Three Citrons" version.

If we only had the version by Romero to investigate, it would not be inappropriate to hypothesize that, given the way the main characters are presented, the most important premise of this story could be the absence of or the weakened state of the feminine element. Also, it may portray a kind of psychic economy in which what had prevailed so far, that is, the masculine principle, is exhibiting signs of exhaustion. Here, the father, having nothing to offer his sons, gives them only watermelons for their journey, necessary for them in order to take possession of their own lives.

The figure of this father in the fairytale should not, however, be understood as a personal father figure, for it is an archetypal image. In Romero's version, the father carries the value normally attributed to the figure of the king. This means that he is the dominant principle in the tale, thus he is responsible for giving the necessary leadership and support to maintain an elemental order that holds life together. It seems obvious that this principle is showing signs of decay, and is no longer able to provide the sons with sufficient energy to maintain the *status quo*.

When the king in the fairytale, who embodies the regulatory and dominant principle of collective life, shows signs that he can no longer respond to the demands inherent to his rank, there occurs a movement towards the renewal of this principle. In archaic societies, since the king was seen as the representative and regulator of natural forces, regicide was a common practice, as a call for the rejuvenation of such powers. The aging of the king, or "his failure" to maintain the dynamism required to support life, represented a threat of collapse for the entire nation.

The declaration *"The king is dead, long live the king"* clearly conveys the esteemed value of such a creative and regulatory principle, indispensable for the existential meaning it provides for the social group. Therefore, the king who has lost his potency must be replaced immediately.[14] So, it is understandable that in Romero's and in Guimarães' versions of the tale, the sons and the prince respectively, must leave or have already left their home in search of something which would be meaningful for their lives. This reinforces the above-mentioned hypothesis, that the masculine principle is progressively weakening while the feminine principle is lacking and, in some way, suppressed.

Psychologically speaking, the initial presentation of the fairytale is equivalent to those moments in life when the individual goes through a process of meaninglessness, that is, the Ego somehow lacks a sense of existential worth. In the normal development of a human being, it is necessary in the first half of life that the Ego adopts a one-sided attitude in order to come to terms with the collective demands of life. During this time, individuals must grapple with societal values that dictate an imperative to achieve all those things that qualify as *goods necessary to be obtained*. In order to adapt, all libido is made available to the Ego for the necessary process of "identifying" personal values within collective ways of life. So, a certain individual essence is sacrificed in adherence to outer demands. There is a hypertrophy of Ego consciousness and a smothering of symbolic life.

But once the individual reaches a certain age or has managed to achieve most of the prerogatives imposed by collective living, a period of great psychic aridity may set in; life appears to stagnate. Usually, depressive processes break in or just intensify, and there arises a deep need to delve into one's own personal essence. This is a moment of crisis for the Ego, which with its one-sided and extroverted world view finds it difficult to deal with the demands of inner life. Or, put in another way, now it is the soul that imposes itself on the individual and takes over the personality. It is his or her inner life which demands to be heard, in place of external or collective demands. The individual, who may have overlooked many important issues of his or her inner life, now may find himself or herself in a state of profound internal stagnation. All that has

---

[14] M.-L. von Franz, *The interpretation of Fairytales*, 127.

been suppressed or repressed, although of vital importance to his or her personal psychic economy, is now pressing to be heard.

In the other versions examined here, there seems to be a certain balance between the masculine and feminine principles, for the king and the queen are present. However, the situation is not totally stable, since we find a son who is reluctant to marry or establishes complicated conditions to accept marriage. Examining this initially from the numerical point of view, it is evident that something is still "lacking" in these versions. For example:

a) In Romero's tale we find a quaternion made up solely of masculine figures; therefore, the feminine element is missing;

b) In Guimarães' version, there is a male representative who lives on "earth" and a female counterpart who lives in the fantastical realm. So here we have an already established couple, but not as a real match. It lacks the earthy feminine counterpart to the prince, as well as the masculine pairing in the fairy dreamworld;

c) In the Bél Princess version, there are eight masculine figures (a king plus seven sons) and seven feminine figures (a queen and six daughters-in-law). It lacks the eighth feminine figure to complete the two quaternions;

d) In "The Three Citrons" tale, the queen appears only at the very end of the tale. All development is based on the figures of the father and the son who are in conflict;

e) In the version of "The Love of the Three Oranges," there is a ternary: a king, a queen and a "dumb" prince. The fourth element, which should be feminine to complete the two pairs, is evidently missing. But even though the masculine is prevalent, it is portrayed as somehow weakened. It is the same situation as found in "The Love of the Three Pomegranates."

Thus, the study of these other variants elucidates another aspect to be investigated. In addition to the weakness of the masculine principle and the limited inclusion of the feminine, there is also something wrong with the attitude of the prince. He resists uniting with the feminine, or he makes the prospect of such union difficult. It is possible to suggest, therefore, that in this tale the masculine principle suffers from a very neurotic condition. We will explore this condition later on, but for now it should be made clear that the depotentiation of the masculine in these tales is so great that it cannot call up the energy to revitalize itself. As it is pointed out in "The Love of the Three Oranges," the queen even requests the lord's intervention in favor of her son who, besides being not so intelligent, cannot laugh. This gives us an idea of how much sorrow hovers around the prince, and that nothing is able to "animate" him.

In "The Three Citrons" version, we find a more dramatic description of the intransigence of the son and the despair of his father. It is stated that the prince was "*so obstinately against marriage that whenever the subject of getting married was brought up, he changed the subject, shook his head, and wished to be hundreds of miles away from there.*"

So an additional hypothesis could be proposed, that the masculine principle as it appears in the story, is not only psychically impoverished but, also, clearly demonstrates a maladjustment to social life, which is then a clear demonstration of a neurotic condition. In this case, it is, therefore, necessary to investigate why the tale portrays the prince with these conditions.

Knowing that fairytales, generally speaking, are narratives which emerge as compensations for the collective psychic economy, one could ask to what the prince's neurotic display is pointing. What does it mean? What led the prince to present as a fool, feeling sad and unwilling to consider marriage?

As we have no specific associations for a more adequate investigation of these questions, it is at least possible to say that such a presentation reflects a deep alienation within the prince. He fails to conform to outer expectations and is perceived as or acts like a fool, irritated and melancholic. Besides, he is unable to fulfill the expected development of a man, that is, to find a woman and to engender. He therefore lacks a certain *élan vital*, a condition very characteristic of an existential crisis typical of neurotic processes, where the individual is cut off from his inner sources of value. Actually, when we move away from our instincts, or overly "domesticate" them in order to establish our civilized life, a conflict between our inner essence and the demands imposed on us by outer life sets in.

Considering that such tales, especially the European versions, were probably structured under the aegis of Christianity, it does not seem implausible to say that what was going on in the background of the psyche was a progressive distancing of man from his instincts, while the feminine principle was still under suppression. As mentioned above, the first records of both the Portuguese and the Italian versions date back to the sixteenth and seventeenth centuries. Before this time, a more differentiated feeling relationship toward women was initiated in men, in the form of Courtly Love. But this movement was soon repressed by the Church, out of concern that it would loosen the sacred bonds of marriage. This then would affect the number of children begotten out of marriage, could create inheritance issues, and so forth. Men were then forced to tame their biological urges and project the ideal feminine onto the spiritual image of the Virgin Mary, a split form of the feminine that is too pure, remote, immaculate and distant from the instincts. This was a significant historical moment, considering that the emerging revaluing of the feminine and of women in general now once again became dissociated and denied. The chthonic, earthy and biological aspects of the feminine were bottled up, repressed, and finally crushed through the witch hunts around the sixteenth century. Therefore, these tales probably originated sometime after the Troubadours and before the Enlightenment, the latter being the historical time during which there occurred a progressive sedimentation of man's energy in the field of ideas. From the social point of view, the prince could represent the image of someone who finds himself caught up between the opposites, that is, his essence as a biological being is in a progressive process of spiritualization.

In the two Italian versions "The Love of the Three Pomegranates" and "The Three Citrons," the prince who has been reluctant to marry only accepts the idea of finding a woman after an accident in which he cuts his finger. While gazing upon the red of the blood and the white of the cheese (in other versions, milk), he has an insight. This is an interesting moment from the point of view of psychic dynamics, for it illustrates the power of "images" in coagulating a condition we experience within. When a given outer image coincides with an intra-psychic process, that is to say, when a synchronistic event occurs, there is a chance that inner conflicts will find an outlet so that they can evolve and eventually be resolved. It is important to point out that the practice of writing down, painting or playing with the images that are offered to us in dreams or visions, or from other experiences emerging from the unconscious, is strongly encouraged in Jungian psychology, exactly because of this power to coagulate our inner dramas. Coagulation here should be understood as embodiment, bringing an idea into a tridimensional realization, that is, as existing in time and space.

So, as soon as the juxtaposition of the red of the blood and the white of the cheese/milk are realized, these images emulate the very conflict the prince is struggling within, that is, the difficulty to conciliate the opposites inside himself. He finally manages to declare that he will only take a wife, as long as she is *as white as cheese and as red as blood.* In other words, the prince is in search of an image capable of harmonizing the opposition he experiences subjectively. This important event in the fairytale reveals that the prince is trapped between two inner opposing forces, illustrating that his being is held captive by a neurotic condition. This is an impossible situation, as his parents emphasize by saying that *"what is red cannot be white, and what is white cannot be red."*

It is important to say that the prince only utters this verdict after being deeply impressed subjectively by an external event occurring to his body. This has great symbolic value for, in this case, the "healing" of his neurosis begins with an experience with the body, an important vehicle through and by which the unconscious may also be constellated. That is, through the body, something which at first had only been thought of, may eventually become brought to reality. Obviously, this is not a new finding, since psychological literature is full of cases in which one may find vast references relating deep psychic changes catalyzed by physical illnesses, accidents or traumas. A patient who spent some time in the hospital due to a serious illness reported feeling complete and inexorable submission to medical procedures and to the health professionals who attended her. By losing control over her body, over her personal autonomy and having her modesty exposed, she had but to "trust" something; she really had to surrender herself. She had to deliver herself to the supposition that everything was part of a plan for her recovery. In other words, she found herself disarmed and deprived of all her beliefs, codes, opinions and attitudes, hoping that the Self would act prospectively at that moment. She had no other solution but to surrender her crystallized Ego, to sacrifice and to trust in a help which went beyond her intellectual control. In other words, she had but to let it happen!

In the specific case of this fairytale, a wound occurred to the prince's finger. This suggests that the unconscious has utilized a cut in the exact structure (the finger) related to manipulation. Symbolically, it could be understood that the unconscious severs the prince's psychic tendency to manipulate and indulge himself in idealistic reveries, in order to prepare him to fulfill his duties as a man. The prince's state of immobility could only be altered when something began to flow from himself. The objective experience of a cut indicates, symbolically, a first step towards the disentanglement from the opposites. Through this "accident," the prince brought energy in, brought Eros (he bled!) into a condition which could only be transformed through the sacrifice of this kind of Ego disposition as depicted by his manipulative behavior. It is as if, now, the problem got under the prince's skin. As Barbara Hannah recalls, it is only when we sacrifice what is most precious to us that we can expect the complexes to lose their hold on us, and alleviate the autonomy and autocratic power they hold over us.[15]

Beyond his resistance to matrimony, the prince reveals further evidence of a neurotic state in his inability to smile; rather he is peevish and obstinate. Lack of humor and vitality are typical states of individuals who are distanced from their instincts or from

---

[15] B. Hannah, *The Inner Journey: Lectures and Essays on Jungian Psychology*.

symbolic life. Such symptoms reflect a stiffening of the personality which is represented literally in fairytale whenever, for instance, a character is transformed into a marble statue or stone. Such individuals become crystallized in a given time and space, waiting for a redeeming symbol.

Absence of humor, or even of bad humor, are unmistakable indicators that the Ego is not anchored in the Self. In such situations a profound lack of harmony is observable, concerning the relationship between the individual and his soul, that is, his "Anima." A man like this lacks *élan vital*, is fragile and eventually succumbs to sentimentalities; he becomes a victim of his own emotions. He is quite often ambivalent in his positions, opinions and actions towards life. It is worth saying that humor, from the psychological point of view, must be understood as the capability to have an extended view of matters. It is a kind of "consciousness beyond consciousness." Humor enables one to go beyond what is already perceptible and transforms a sometimes rough situation into something laughable. Only when the Ego functions under the auspices of the Self does one gain the ability to reshape constraining challenges and to relativize the oppressive issues in one's relationships.

Nonetheless — and this is very important — one must consider the prospective possibility within neurosis. The confinement in which the individual eventually finds himself due to such a psychic condition may be the only outlet capable of allowing him to ward off the excessive luring and demands of what is considered a "normal," desirable or expected social life. It is as if the purpose of the neurosis is to put the individual "on hold" until a new redeeming symbol is formed, so that his libido may flow beyond social adaptation. Only then may he reach the inner core of his being and flourish as a real individual. Therefore, the neurosis is also (or almost always) an anticipation or the "kick off" of the individuation process. Marie-Louise von Franz has asserted that some neurotic processes or depressive periods ought also to be seen as a protective mechanism for the individual.[16] In this way, the neurosis of the prince might reflect the necessity for protection against the abusive requests from collective life and from the mere repetition of social demands imposed upon him. From the clinical point of view, this is an important consideration to understand, for within a depressive state may hide a creative core, eager to be lived out.

Therefore, from out of this neurotic state a new symbol arises, which not only depicts the problem but also indicates the way out of it. The red and the white colors emulate an opposing situation, which, first, seems impossible to solve from the objective point of view. On the other hand, this image establishes a goal for the prince who, instead of remaining lost within himself, chooses a *quête d l'âme* (quest of the soul). In a way, the path that opens up before him appears to be as neurotic as the neurosis which generated it, since it seems impossible, but it is the only possible solution. This kind of journey can only be explained in light of the "instinct pull," for this is exactly how the unconscious proposes a solution towards reconciliation of the opposites — through the irrational.

It is worth remembering that the cut to the prince's finger occurs at the moment when he is eating. From the psychic point of view, it means that he was involved in the symbolical enacting of his nourishing habits, that is, the meal table of his domesticated social life, or the domesticated daily food offered by the society he lives in. But now the unconscious has cut it off.

In the Indian version of "The Bél Princess" the prince's behavior is further colored by the fact that he not only despises his six sisters-in-law but also refuses to *"receive food from their hands."* Thus, it seems that time has come for the prince to break away. He can no longer adapt to or be nourished by the prevailing social setup. From the practical point of view, this man needs not only to find his woman but also, above all, it illustrates that, as an individual, he must come to terms with his soul — that is, with the Anima. And for that matter, he must cut himself off from his domestic entanglements.

---

[16] M.-L. von Franz, *Interprétation du conte d'Apulée: L'âne d'or,* La Fontaine de Pierre 4ᵉ ed., 88.

THE COLORS OF BLOOD AND CHEESE

From a symbolic point of view, red usually represents an emotionally intense and vital human experience. In the above case, the red color comes from blood, another element connected to life, instinct, passion and sensuality. However, on the other hand, there is a destructive aspect in red and blood, as linked to aggressiveness, despair and fury. Both Mars and Venus are associated with this color. But in the specific case of this tale, the red blood comes from a cut in the finger, that is, a symbolic cut in one of the manipulating "tools" of the prince — his finger.

Now, white, representing the absorption of all colors, is not even considered a color itself. It is usually classified as a "non-color" or else a fusion of all of them. In our Western hemisphere, white is primarily associated with purity, absence of feelings or emotions, or even death. Here in Brazil, when it is said that someone has gone red with anger, everyone understands how intense this feeling is and the damage that could come out of it. But if one says that the person turned "white with anger" (pale), it sounds like ice; it is livid, and the reaction is not so evident. But there remains a feeling that something worse, even deadly, may occur. In China, India and Japan, white is the color of mourning. Therefore, it is associated with transition, a change from one state to another, life/death, immortality, but also annihilation. On the other hand, white is the color of salt, of Eros, that which gives taste to food, and in the case we are dealing with, the color of cheese or milk. Milk is a liquid that nurtures, especially in the first stages of development. So, in the specific tale, it seems to be connected with the provision of life and the change of status.

Whatever it may be said about the positive and negative qualities of these two colors, one must remember that this is but an attempt to categorize what could be associated with them. The truly essence of their meaning is forever concealed. Nevertheless, these classifications are important while analyzing this fairytale, for they help us in mapping the neurotic path through which the characters of the tale go through in the course of their development. We are talking here about a man belonging to a time where a progressive spiritualization was going on, not only in the mystical sense, but intellectually speaking. That is, we see a progressive domestication of his instinctual life. Therefore, the investigation of these two colors clarifies the conflict before him. The emergence of this pair of colors helps us to envision two opposing directions in this man's life, both undeniably possibilities to come into reality. If he just sits and allows himself to become mesmerized by them, he may just succumb to his neurosis. But if he follows what this pair is heralding, he may well fulfill his destiny.

The table below is a modest attempt to sort out the attributes usually ascribed to the colors:

Red		White	
Positive	Negative	Positive	Negative
Life	Anger	Purity	Annihilation
Passion	Luxury	Innocence	Absence of color
Sensuality	Destruction	Transition	Coldness
Love	Hell	Life	Death
Warmness	Aggressiveness	Eros	Impersonality

When the prince finds himself paralyzed inside his neurosis, cuts his finger and faces the redness and the whiteness in front of him, it is as if such an image emulates the conditions he experiences within himself. At this moment, the image breaks through his psyche and the state of inner immobility is then fortunately interrupted. This situation is extremely important in analytical practice, for it illustrates the power the concretized image — that is the iconographic crystallization of a given symbol — can have on the psychic functions of an individual. Through the materialization of a given symbol, it is as if a communication between the image and the internal personal psychic processes can be established. This is an old assertion already known by the ancient philosophers, who understood the existence of idols as a way of embodiment of man's thoughts, wishes, and ideas. Such a materialization provides an opportunity to spur a dialogue between the image/icon and its interlocutor. Also, considering that such images emanate from the Self, the communication between the image and the individual actually becomes a conversation between the Unconscious and Ego. Consequently, at this moment the prince now understands what he is longing for — a condition of wholeness where the opposites can be harmonized.

Another association for these two colors can be derived from the alchemical process. Following the transformation or resolution of Chaos, represented by the *nigredo*, there comes the stage of *albedo* (white), where there is a certain organization of the opposing and destructive forces formerly present in the state of blackness. However, if the transformation process is to be continued, there must be libido in it. That is, there must be life in that which has just undergone transformation. Nobody can live in a state of permanent whiteness, as something abstract, only as an idea, which has not yet been realized. That would be but just an innocent conclusion of matters. Hence, life must be injected at this moment; there must be a flow of blood at this stage, so that existence comes into being. What follows then is the *rubedo* phase, which represents exactly the moment when vital energy and emotion are added. In analysis, for example, the process cannot be realized without feeling and emotion. Only with the experience of a full existence can one change the idealistic state of albedo into a robust manner of existing, and for this to occur, blood, energy, passion, fire and love must be introduced into the albedo. As Jung says: "...

> in this state of 'whiteness' one does not live in the true sense of the word, it is a sort of abstract, ideal state. In order to make it come alive it must have 'blood', it must have what the alchemists call the rubedo, the 'redness' of life. Only the total experience of being can transform this ideal state of the albedo into a fully human mode of existence. Blood alone can reanimate a glorious state of consciousness in which the last trace of blackness is dissolved, in which the devil no longer has an autonomous existence but rejoins the profound unity of the psyche.

Then the opus magnum is finished: the human soul is completely integrated."[17]

In the book *Hypnerotomachia Poliphili*, written in the fifteenth century by a Dominican monk, there is a description of Poliphilo's vision about a rite performed by Venus and her companions at the grave/fount of Adonis. In the morning they pick up blooming roses which were still white. Cupid takes the blood and tears the goddess shed upon Adonis' death and, at this moment, all the white roses in the arbor turn red. This reddening of the roses is an indication that Adonis should rise again.[18] So, here, we have another amplification that the red of the blood, understood as emotion, feeling and love investment, is what may reawaken a life worth living.

This interplay of colors can also be found in other fairytales or myths. In "Snow White," for example, the story begins with the Queen Mother who, while standing framed by the black ebony of her window, pricks her finger on a needle, and three drops of red blood fall on the white snow outside. She then wishes to have a daughter who could bear these three colors in herself.

In this tale, the Queen Mother knows she is ill, and that means, from a symbolic point of view, that whatever she represents must be renewed. The Queen also knows that such a rejuvenation is only possible under the auspices of another principle capable of bringing about transformation, represented there by the interplay between the black, white and red colors. In the Greek myth about the disappearance and death of Glaucus, the idea of transformation and rejuvenation can also be seen through the dynamics of these three colors. In the myth, Glaucus may only be found and returned to his father by the person who devises the most suitable comparison to a cow, which continually alternates the colors black, red and white, during the day. The

---

[17] C. G. Jung, *C. G. Jung Speaking: Interviews and Encounters*, eds. William McGuire & R.F.C. Hull, 228.
[18] L. David-Fierz & M. Hottinger, *The Dream of Poliphilo*, 169.

answer to this riddle would be a blackberry which alludes to their maturation process.

In both tales above mentioned, the chaining up of the colors points to a process that leads to the idea of transformation which, consequently, links to the regeneration or renewal.

It is, then, important to point out that at the same time the tale brings up the prince's troubles – his lack of energy, willpower and his neurotic behavior – it also delineates the path which must be taken. On the one hand, the white of the milk (or cheese) reflects his lifeless childish demeanor, his feebleness and virginal innocence, so far linked to the domestic environment. On the other hand, this whiteness also points to maturation, as milk which transforms into cheese, that is, a nutrient typically fed to infants which may undergo processing to become food for more mature individuals. This would be a transformation experience in a man's life which would likely to occur mostly through the relationship to the feminine, although, in this case, still projected so far off. The cut in the prince's finger can be seen as a crisis, and the blood flowing from there indicates his passion not yet lived and the anguish built up due to a meaningless life. With the blood flow, there is an emulation of his erotic potentiality, that is, his capability to socialize and to establish bonds.

In the Indian version, "The Bél Princess," there is a passage in which the prince is transformed into stone. This happens because he fails to follow the instructions given by the fakir. The figure of the fakir in this fairytale is somehow peculiar. He was the first "person" the prince met after he left his parents' home and marched into the unconscious journey. Fakirs are known by their ability, among others, to master their bodily needs and to maintain a very ascetic kind of life. They are extremely spiritual beings, and some of them even levitate, for their bodies are too lean and they feed on "air." This fakir is said to spend half of the year sleeping and the other half awake. It means that part of the time he is in "this world," and the other part he is in the "other world." This makes him a sort of psychopomp, an intermediator between consciousness and unconsciousness. Accordingly, he has mercurial features for he not only teaches tricks to the prince so that he can overcome the difficulties during his quest for the Bél Princess, but he also can contact God to intercede in favor of this young man. So, he is a figure in the service of the Self. And because the fakir is the epitome of instinct control and over- spiritualization, we could think of him as an exacerbation of the prince's features, but in a more positive way, since the Self is his master, not the neurosis which, up to then, had been the suzerain of the prince. Thus, the fakir appears here as the Self concealed under the shadowy aspects, not yet integrated, in the prince. The prince is too spiritualized and too much in control of his instincts, but in a negative fashion for it leads to stagnation of life. Consequently, before the prince can get any help from the fakir, he is supposed to work for some time and also to wait on him.

The rendering of services to a supernatural being met in the wood (in the unconscious) is a very well-known motif found in fairytales, for it is like a training or initiation into the ordeals to come. Somehow, the prince is supposed to learn from the fakir not only devotion to the Self, that is, the surrendering to a high power, but also, how to master his instincts under the auspices of the Self in order to be able to conquer what he is searching for. The mastering here is a kind of willpower but completely different from stubbornness. He needs discipline; he needs to overcome his inertia. He must strive, but anchored in the Self. Of course, every time the prince fails to integrate the fakir's teaching, he succumbs, but fortunately is helped again. A spoiled child is always opinionated and stubbornly attached to his or her own wishes (ideas), yet when it comes to action (fulfilling a task), laziness and tantrums are usually what one encounters when dealing with the immature.

Eventually, our hero ended up petrified; he became rigid, and paralyzed. That is, his neurotic traits were exacerbated at this moment. In this version, not only was the prince affected, but his horse as well. This aspect of his instincts responsible for conducting him through life – the horse – was also turned into a statue. He could no longer master his instincts properly, per say, so whatever he may have learned while staying with the fakir still needed to be experienced in his own way. And again, this situation was only remedied when the fakir cut his own little finger and made the blood flow over the prince and his horse. Then, they could regain their lives once more.

Consulting different fairytale versions is always enriching as it allows for a wider understanding of the dynamics the various elements cast, which are often repeated across them. The cut in the prince's finger as seen in "The Love of the Three Pome-granates" and in "The Three Citrons" versions is completely different from the fakir's version present in "The Bél Princess," for example. In the former two, the situation is like an accident, as it were a metaphor for the need to bring to an end the manipulative and neurotic disposition of the prince. But in the latter, the cut is not accidental, rather, it is purposeful and assigned to a specific finger. Again, we have more evidence to strengthen the hypothesis that the fakir holds analogous aspects, yet in the prince these function negatively.

Symbolically, these two images are very instructive since the way the Self acts in the former is like a synchronistic event. Something had been cooked up in the unconscious without too much participation of the Ego. There is an innominate distress present in the Ego, which is caught between the constellation within the Unconscious and the outer event. The Self just imposes a task to the Ego. But in the fakir's case, the cut seems to be a parcel of all the healing resources available within the psyche. Again, the fakir is himself one aspect of the Self that acts prospectively and, therefore, cures. And it may be quite probable that this cooperative disposition be related to the fact that the prince, as the pre-figuration of an Ego in the story, was more assertive as far as his destiny was concerned; that is, by working under the fakir's tutelage, he may have incorporated something of him. He took an important step towards resolving his previous neurotic behavior. At this point in the fairytale, it is illustrated that the hero (the model for the Ego functioning) was able to make a connection with the deeper layers of the psyche. And by doing so, these deep layers feed back this Ego disposition.

Moreover, there is an indication that the fakir cut a specific finger, the little one. This finger is associated with Hermes, the psychopomp, and, therefore, to the principle of life. In one version about the death of Attis, it is said that he did not undergo an ordinary death, for his body did not corrupt. And this could be asserted by the fact that his hair continued to grow and that he could move his little finger, after his "death."[19] Also, there is a legend about Isis who restored the health of the dangerously ill baby Dictys of Biblos, son of the Queen Astarte, by giving him her little finger to suck, instead of her breast.

As far as the little finger is concerned, it is always amazing to witness the timeless power of an archetype, seen by a recurrent dream motif told to me recently. A woman said that she often has dreams of being suffocated while sleeping. This terrifies her tremendously, and she wakes up feeling she may die. But, interesting enough, while she was still dreaming, she "learned" that if she could manage to wiggle her little finger she would "know" that she was after all only dreaming and that she was not going to die. She continues to have these dreams currently, but now she knows how to mitigate her lack of air and feeling of dying. Of course, the meaning of the dream is still not grasped, for it continues to occur!

It is interesting to see that, in English, the little finger is called *"pinky finger."* Pinky here, etymologically speaking, derives from Dutch, which means little finger. But one may be seduced to think further, considering that the pink color is the blend between red and white. This is the bringing together of the opposition so fundamental to keeping the flow of life moving! There is an alchemical reference to the Stone of Sages because pink represents the goal of the alchemist in bringing together the opposites: the union between white (feminine) and red (masculine).[20]

Therefore, the fact that the fakir deliberately made blood flow from this specific finger is suggestive that life is being given back. Such cooperative dynamics between Self and Ego is a commonly observed psychological principle which occurs whenever an

---

[19] R.B. Onians, *The Origins of European Thought,* 110.
[20] T. Abt, *Introduction to Picture Interpretation According to C.G. Jung.*

individual fully embraces his own personal task; at this moment the nurturing resources lodged in the deeper strata of the psyche flow back again. This is what Edinger pointed out as the reestablishing of the Ego/Self axis.[21]

This way, by projecting the positive values of both the red and the white on a place or, more specifically, on a still non-existent woman, he begins to feel an urge to go out into the world in search for himself, through the figure of a princess. The blood falls into his milk, the still infantile nourishment (or on its derivative, already transformed by human conscience — cheese). It is, therefore, from within the prince himself that the impulse of life emerges. The accident — the unconscious — sacrifices his finger and from there flows the redness that will hopefully impregnate his existence, up to now still fettered to the domestic sphere.

Hence, when the prince declares he wishes to marry a woman as red as blood and as white as milk, there is a projection of the solution to this conflict on an image difficult to be achieved, as it cannot be found in any known place. It must be emphasized, however, that what has been called *neurotic* about his inner experience is only so when what is prevailing is the state of immobility, that is, while the opposing forces keep the prince separated from the sources of life, thus impeding his libido from finding a proper outlet. Jung highlights the vital aspect of such a dynamic — that is, the play of the opposites — by saying that life could not exist without the presence of the opposites, and therefore *"the opposing pairs should not be looked upon as mistakes, but as the origin of life."*[22] Neurosis here may only be named so while the prince remains in that inner conflict and the flow of life is blocked. As soon as the symbol appears, instead of the conflict there is a problem to be solved. Consequently, conflict and problem are separate aspects the individual eventually faces in his lifetime. But the differentiation between these two instances is necessary because the way they evolve is specific to each other. The former may lead to immobility, a psychic stagnation, while the

---

[21] E. Edinger, *Ego and Archetype*, 6.
[22] C. G. Jung, *Analytical Psychology – Notes on the seminar given in 1925*, 78.

latter to the possibility of finding solution, thus, to psychological development.

The absurdity of the combination of these two colors presented in this fairytale characterizes, therefore, the archetypal image of the elixir, or the "hard to find" motif. In the tale "Psyche and Eros," inserted in novel *The Golden Ass,* written by Lucius Apueius, second century CE, the extra-mundane value of the combination of these two colors can be seen when Psyche realizes the divinity of her husband, Eros, by seeing the white-reddy neck and cheeks.[23]

Considering then that the elixir of these fairytales is related to the feminine, it strengthens the hypothesis that the main problem with these stories is related to the masculine principle. As said, we do not know for sure the exact time these tales appeared, but we may have a glimpse of how old the usage of such a motif is by the historical record obtained through the Troubadours' songs. The "Cantiga da Ribeirinha," one of the first literary texts written in Gaelic-Portuguese, dated to the year of 1189, tells of the platonic love of a man by his unattainable beloved and makes use of the combination of these two colors to characterize it: [24]

> *"In world nobody is similar to myself,*
> *while my life keeps going as things go,*
> *because I die for you, and oh!*
> *my lady **of white skin and reddish face**,*
> *you desire that I describe you*
> *when I saw you without mantle*
> *Cursed day! I got up*

---

[23] Videt capitis aurei genialem caesariem ambrosia temulentam, cervices lacteas genasque purpureas pererrantes crinium globos decoriter impeditos, alios antependulos, alios retropendulos, quorum splendore nimio fulgurante iam et ipsum lumen lucernae vacillabatAPVLEIVS. (c. A.D. 123/5 – c. 180). Metamorphoses http://www.thelatinlibrary.com/apuleius/apuleius5.shtml April 10, 2013.

[24] http://linguaportuguesapb.blogspot.com/2011/03/cantiga-da-ribeirinha.html March 1, 2012.

and no more saw you ugly!
And, my lady, since that day, ow
everything goes very badly for me
and you, daughter of don Father
Moniz, and it really seems for you
that I received from you a mantle
but I, my lady, as a gift,
have never received
something, even a worthless one."

So, when the prince says that now he is apt to go out in search for his red and white bride, he declares that he is after the symbol of unification, redemption and transcendence. That is, he begins a quest of the soul towards the Self, and under the auspices of the Self.

Notwithstanding, if we consider the alchemical development, it can be observed that the sequencing of colors in the tale is not presented in the usual manner. Why is it that the black color does not appear explicitly in in the prince's surrounding?

As a matter of fact, the *nigredo* situation, although not having been openly spoken in the tale, is depicted in the very situation of the prince. Neurosis is a moment of extreme disorder for the human being. The prince is in a condition where life is stagnant, a state of *massa confusa*, as the alchemists would say. As already described above, his life is at a standstill; he feels out-of-place, confused and neurotic. It is a situation comparable to that of the Queen Mother in "Snow White," when she is *"framed in her window of black ebony"* thinking about her illness. In the view of the alchemists, this state of *massa confusa*, of *melanosis* (nigredo) can only be conquered through a process of mortification, separation or severing. Beating, decaying, quartering or beheading are some of the images used by the alchemists to represent a way to free the spirit from its imprisonment within the decayed matter, so that the process of transformation may continue. This way the nigredo process in our fairytale— as it is understood by the alchemists' teachings — is demonstrated by the prince's state of alienation and immobility that is symbolically disrupted by the cut to his finger. Thence, injury to the finger is a clear reference to the matter "prince" going through a mortification process necessary for the transformation of his nigredo condition.

Continuing with the premise of the impoverishment of the masculine in these tales, we can also emphasize the fact that the food the princes or sons receive is very poor in terms of nourishment, as compared to what is normally provided by the father, which is usually the meat obtained from hunting. In Romero, watermelons are offered; in the tale by Guimarães, it is not even the father who provides the food, but the fairy godmother who offers quinces instead. In other versions, the fruit can be oranges, lemons, pomegranates, citrons, apples, walnuts, etc.

As Romero's tale goes on, the watermelons are given with the warning that they should be opened only where there is water. The two eldest sons, however, cannot wait until they come close to a fountain before opening their fruit. From inside, one beautiful lady comes out each time, asking for water or milk. The young men are unable to satisfy their wish, and the ladies disappear. But the youngest son manages to wait for the right moment, and so the tale continues, allowing us to learn about the development of his relationship to the beautiful lady. It should be noted that in all versions there is a clear idea that the prince must only open the fruit near to a water source, for the lady who appears from inside is thirsty. In other words, she is herself eager to be realized. This theme will be taken up further ahead.

Firstly, it is necessary to point out the numerical dynamics quite typical in fairytales. Here, the first youth fails, and so does the second; but the third (usually the youngest, with less experience, inferior in both his masculinity and intellect masculine or intellectually inferior) achieves the expected results, and then the tale goes on. Hence, we have the repetition of the number three, which is symbolically associated with development and progress, and is, in this manner, calling for the fourth incident that will close the sequence of actions.

In the other above-mentioned versions, we do not see three brothers or princes involved with fruit. Instead, there is just one prince who will enact the opening of three fruits. Again, it is only in the third cutting act that he learns (or he recalls) how to prevent the lady from disappearing.

As said, the motif of a fruit that hides a feminine creature within is old and quite prevalent. In the Japanese tale "Uriki-hime" (the Melon Princess), for example, it is said that a melon floating on the river came towards an elderly woman, who picked it up and took it home to share it with her husband. When they cut the melon, out came a beautiful lady. What would then be the psychological meaning of finding a feminine figure in a fruit and the indication that her rescue is only possible by the water?

THE WATER ELEMENT

This is a difficult question to answer! But what all fairytales have in common is the fact that, in principle, these fruits are quite juicy and full of seeds. We have demonstrated on other occasions that water, as one of the most widely known symbols representing the unconscious, is connected with the feminine. So, it would be their "'natural" milieu. Water is considered to be *"the living essence of the psyche,"* and the alchemists created various expressions to designate this water. As pointed out by Marie-Louise von Franz, they called it *"aqua nostra, succus lunarie, mercuris vivus, argentums vivum, vinum ardens, aqua vitae"* and so on. With these names, the alchemists meant the water was a *"living being, not without substance, different from the rigid immateriality of the mind in abstract."*[25]

In the mythology of Candomblé (an African Brazilian religion), for example, the domain of the waters, be they pluvial (rain), fluvial (rivers) or maritime (sea), belongs to the goddesses: Iemanjá (mistress of the great waters, oceans and seas), Oxum (mistress of fresh water), Iansã (mistress of rainstorms), Obá (ruler of river rapids) and Euá (goddess of the springs). In Christianity, grottos with water springs are often utilized as small altars to dispense

---

[25] M.-L. von Franz, *Dreams – A Study of the Dreams of Jung, Descartes, Socrates, and Other Historical Figures.*

offerings to the Virgin Mary and other saints of the Catholic pantheon. Besides, the source of all creation is water considering that every reproduction system needs it; be it in the form of the open waters as the oceans, lakes or rivers, or within enclosed environments such as the eggs or pouches containing the amniotic liquid found in many higher vertebrates. This way, the image of the feminine cannot be separated from the waters, so the appearance of a princess from inside a fruit can be understood in this light.

There is however another important aspect in all versions we examined, which is the fact that the prince must open the fruit only near to a water source. This is because the princess is so thirsty that if she is not quenched immediately, she may perish.

So far, we have highlighted the importance of the waters as the great originator of life. Anytime the scientists are searching for life on other planets, what they look for primarily is whether there is any trace of water in that place. However, it is important to say that water also contains a regenerating and vivifying capacity. In Egypt, images of the dead lying in subterranean caves waiting for the resurrection waters date from time immemorial. In the *Dialogue of Cleopatra and the Philosophers*, Cleopatra, an alchemist belonging to the school of Mary the Prophetess, says to the philosophers: *"waters, when they come near, awaken the bodies and the souls that are imprisoned and weak..."*[26] In the Bible, we find another passage which refers to the curing power of Bethesda waters: *"the first sick person to enter the pool after the water was stirred up would recover from whatever disease had afflicted him"* (John 5:4). This stirring of the water means the intercession of the Holy Spirit. In Jung, we can read that *"water is described as an elixir of life which awakens the dead from their sleep in Hades to enter a new springtime."*[27] There are several other fairytales in which the main quest is for *"the water from the fountain of life"* to restore the king's health, who is seriously ill. In this context, therefore, water is equal to the concept of the Self, in Jungian analytic psychology.

---

[26] J. Lindsay, *The Origins of Alchemy in Graeco-Roman Egypt,* 254.
[27] C. G. Jung, *Alchemical Studies,* CW 13, §103.

There is another allusion in the Gospel of John (John 4:7-30) which is very instrumental in this sense, especially because it expands even more the specific theme of these tales. This is the meeting of Jesus with the Samaritan woman at Jacob's well. The woman asks Jesus to give to her from the *"living water"* whose power forever quenches the thirst of those who drink from it, and Jesus says, *"Indeed, the water I give them will become in them a spring of water welling up to eternal life."*

Hence, we have two important considerations to make about water at this moment. First, by mentioning these juicy fruits, there is a clear reference to the feminine as belonging to this environment, so this is the place to look for it. Secondly, this feminine element in the tales is thirsty, under the risk of perishing if not vivified through hydration. Water, at this moment, has the power to foster life. The man who opens up the fruit in order to recover the feminine must do so near to water, to satiate the lady's thirst. From a psychological point of view, this means that, first, the feminine is anxious to be acknowledged for she has been kept too long in suppression; and second, she can only be approached by the masculine when considered in her own essence or, better still, if she were welcomed based on her own premises.

When a man gives vivifying water to a lady, it means that he deeply understands her; that he respects, knows and also carries inside himself what is important to a woman. It is not uncommon to observe in the dynamics between couples that there can frequently be found an inclination of one partner to try to make the other become *"the way I like it"* or how it *"pleases me."* This attitude robs the other of his or her individuality, suffocates one's particular qualities and results in a never-ending source of conflicts for both. In the book "Near to the Wild Heart", Clarice Lispector illustrates the issue quite well:

"Otávio made her into something that wasn't her but himself, and Joana received it out of pity for them both, as they both were unable to free themselves through love,

because she, succumbed, accepted her own fear of suffering, her incapability to get herself beyond the frontier of revolt."[28]

The need to relate to a person without overwhelming him or her amply displayed in other fairytales. In the German version of the tale "Water Maid"[29] (Die Wasserjungfer), the need of the feminine to be met on her own terms can be seen. Here, the fisherman rescues a beautiful lady who accepts his proposal of marriage on the stipulation that for one day a week he should not seek her out nor ask any questions about her whereabouts. He complies with this until one day, out of curiosity, he finds her out bathing in a basin. He then discovers that the lower part of her body ends in a fishtail, and then he gets to know her Melusine nature. But once her secret was uncovered, she no longer reassumed her human shape, and then disappeared forever. The husband, together with his handsome children, all died.

Psychologically speaking, what is being portrayed in this fairytale is the absorption of the feminine principle by the unconscious. In man, the psychic function of the feminine, his soul, is represented by the Anima, which, when supported by the Ego, opens up to him a vital connection to the ordering center of the psyche – the Self. In this German tale, we have what is called the *"loss of the soul,"* for the masculine element is unable to suitably welcome the feminine with her particular qualities. From the practical point of view, this is the kind of man who is not capable of trust or is unable fulfill his creative potentiality and mistrusts whatever has had inspired him from within. He allows the opportunity for transformation to escape just because he does not develop a relationship of trust between himself and his creative soul. This is the typical situation of a man under the negative mother complex, who cannot create a nurturing relationship to a woman.

---

[28] C. Lispector, *Perto do Coração Selvagem*, Francisco Alves Ed. 14, 40.
[29] "The Water Maid," http://www.pitt.edu/~dash/melusina.html.

Man's disobliging attitude towards the feminine principle has negative consequences for him, not only externally, as it produces a conflict-laden and tumultuous relationship between man and woman, but also internally, as this disregard can be greatly catastrophic once the man who is split-off from his soul faces a progressive psychic impoverishment and a host of psychic maladies. In the tale, there was a violation of the feminine which amounted to masculine alienation. The situation depicted is even more instructional when one considers that the feminine still needed to return to water even while she was already interacting with her man. This means that even though the man was able to approach the feminine, his Anima, her integration or redemption was not yet complete. That is, the feminine was not adequately unified within consciousness, as she had to return periodically to her non-human shape and to her natural environment. Thus, the caring for such a relationship seemed to be more laborious than simply getting "together." It was necessary that the masculine principle truly honored and respected the difference and peculiarity of his counterpart, the feminine.

But leaving aside the psychology of man, this German tale also teaches us some important lessons regarding the psychology of women and the dynamics of the feminine. Just as above we identified the feminine element related to a man's Ego as his soul/Anima, whose function is to make connection with the Self, in woman's Ego, this link to the Self is made by a masculine element of spiritual nature, which we denominate the Animus. Thus, considering the Melusine image as an allegory for the feminine Ego in process of development, the figure of the husband would be her spirit counterpart, that is, her Animus. The story illustrates an underdeveloped feminine Ego by representing a woman who is still a fish and needs to return periodically to water. This is a symbolic portrayal of the feminine conscience that is still quite unconscious about herself. In the case of man's psychology, this story revealed a masculine Ego succumbing mostly due to his rigidity and incapability of accommodating appropriately the contents of his soul (vanishing of the woman/mermaid).

But in the case of woman's psychology, the feminine Ego is rather immature and, thus, unable to cope with the tasks proposed by her Spirit. In its positive aspect, when in the story the husband fails to respect her need to isolate and to keep her mystery to herself, this can also be understood as an invitation to the feminine Ego to sever its bond to the condition of unconsciousness, that is, her undifferentiation and her archaic traits. From the practical point of view, this may be the kind of woman who lives but to seduce and to enchant men and life in general, and nothing more! She is identified with a *"siren-like"* nature or with the enchanting quality of the unconscious. And as this Ego is still too immature, such an Animus is perceived (and indeed acts!) negatively. Their relationship eventually turns into an obstacle which impedes the woman's development since this association is based on mistrust and lack of harmony with her spiritual potentiality. Therefore, what was genuinely human in the feminine in the tale goes back to the abysmal waters of the unconscious, into its dark and unrealizable aspect. If we said that in man this situation characterizes a loss of soul, in woman it may be seen as mostly the succumb of her Ego.

From the practical point of view, this situation can be seen with wives who cannot free themselves properly from their paternal household, behaving in a dependent manner and longing for caring, as eternal daughters. It is not uncommon to observe many women with this disposition, who end up marrying masculine figures who, instead of being inspiring and edifying, lead them to a progressive obfuscation of their personality and individuality. Unfortunately, this immature feminine Ego is prey for the unconscious and, therefore, is invaded, violated and fated to become psychically ill.

In the "Water Maid," it is necessary that the masculine element promptly recognizes the essence of the feminine and realizes that its flourishment requires its own domain. That is the first requirement for the healing process of the wound caused by the split between the feminine and masculine principles. From man's psychological point of view, it means that the values pertaining to the feminine principle — may they be Eros, welcoming, completeness, accommodation, and so on — should first be rediscovered (removed from the fruit) and then nourished back by these same values. And this means to put them immediately into practice, so that they can be realized based on its own terms. Eros feeds itself on relations; receptiveness is nourished by warmness, and completeness is obtained through inclusion — *similia similibus curantur.*[30]

In Romero's version, the lady asks for water or milk, and this should be understood in a particular way. It suggests that, here, the feminine is still in an initial stage of development in that she may be quenched with milk, a typical food for newborn babies. As a matter of fact, allegorically, this is true for she has just been reborn out of the fruit. As a new-born, then, this new image of the feminine demands care so that she may eventually mature. In ancient times, there was a ritual sacrifice in which milk was offered to the goddess of the underworld and also to the dead. Such sacrifices, called *nephalia*, were carried out to celebrate fertility and rebirth. Thus, milk here is fostering life.

When man, then, starts to relate to his soul, or better, when he becomes conscious of the existence of the Anima function in his psychic economy, zeal, extreme care and dedication will be required of him; for this is the only way that the relationship may grow and prosper. In the "Love of The Three Pomegranates" version, the maiden is naked when she comes out from the fruit, demonstrating the need for protection of this newly discovered content in man's psychology. It can be said further that this maiden goes through different transforming processes, according to the various versions under study, indicating that, functionally, she is always in process of maturation.

Nevertheless, when the prince offers the princess something to drink, the problem of the shadow constellates. The otherwise auspicious blossoming, initially heralded by the appearance of the young damsel, is accompanied by her gloomy aspect. The promising coming together of the two principles still requires intense work with the negative, and even more rejected, aspect of the feminine.

---

[30] "Like things are cured by like."

Here again we have another psychic development which is well delineated in the tale: every time a psychic content is brought up into the light, its shadow is constellated. Therefore, the promise of a prolific, significant and everlasting encounter between prince and princess must take into consideration the corrosive and destructive aspect of the princess' shadow (or the dark Anima of the prince). It is necessary, then, to embrace the demoniac in the feminine.

THE DEMONIC FEMININE

The fact is that the prince eventually has to face the dark side of the feminine: the black principle personified by the Mooress; or the Saracen (in other versions); or the evil sorceress, the Negress. In other words, the prince, up until the time of his meeting with the princess, is not aware of her dark side, here personified by the old, dark-colored servant, who turns out to be a real witch. The exclusion of this shadowy feminine element is a typical attitude within Christian psychology. There, the chthonic principle was removed from the conscious sphere and remained in deep unconsciousness. It is no wonder then that the dark aspect of *"matter"* should produce a vengeful and destructive behavior.

Jung says that with the advent of Christianity, man went through a disruption between spirit and matter. This allowed him to *"not only think beyond Nature, but also in opposition to it … [and] this distancing from the darkness of the depths of Nature ended up in a Trinitarian thought, moving man to a platonic and supra-celestial domain."*[31]

The kingdom of the Father, Son and Holy Ghost thus excludes the mother of the Son-God, the life giver per se. Therefore, the price paid for progressive spiritualization was the buffering of the feminine, which led women and the feminine to become demonic. For the feminine is not only the good goddess, it is also the all-

---

[31] C. G. Jung, *Psychology and Religion,* CW 11, §261.

destructive and all-absorbing element — the crazy mother who devours everything. The main problem with the Christian philosophy, therefore, is that it could not hold together these two aspects of the feminine principle, namely, the life-giving and the life-destructing aspects. And that is what makes things so unbearable. Consequently, it is inevitable that when the prince finds his enlightened princess, she also carries with her an obscure aspect, personified by the Crooked Mooress. From a depth psychology point of view, the meeting between man and his Anima presupposes a "full package"; that is, he cannot go without experiencing both the illuminated and dark sides — the accepted and rejected aspects such a psychic function constellates.

It is then possible to propose a broader hypothesis for the theme of these fairytales when we say that besides the weakening of the masculine, the neurotic behavior of the prince reflects the "demonized" feminine. Hence, considering man's psychodynamics, the tale seems to deal with the question of enfeeblement of the masculine not only because it lacks the integration of the feminine but also because the latter is still in a condition of "damnation."

By analyzing more carefully the Christian catechesis, one may have a better understanding of the demonization of the feminine. We must remember that this religion grew and became strong in a place and time when the cults of the Great Mother were prevalent. In Mediterranean cultures, the most adored divinities were the goddesses associated with earth, water and vegetation, who were often worshipped through rituals including ecstatic practices, sexual orgies and frugality. These rites pertained to chthonic life representing the seasonal interchange between life and death, thus re-enacting cycles of Nature. Therefore, it was not an uncommon practice to act out in a graphic way both the creation and destruction cycles, including not only vegetable or animal sacrifices, but also human immolation.

Life for the Mediterranean man, the one who benefited from the Neolithic revolution, was but a continuum, a contingency, or just a consequence of natural events. Hence, he needed such practices to give symbolic meaning to his existence and not just to succumb to this dynamic of destruction and renewal. In other words, he needed to propitiate the furthering of life. Different from the man who had Christianity well-structured in his psyche, the Pagan was not conscious enough to be able to deal with the undifferentiated energy of the Great Goddesses. The rituals were, then, an attempt to appease the still unconscious powers inherent in such goddesses, which both create and destroy.

From a psychic point of view, the worshipping of the Great Mother in the Mediterranean cultures revealed how uncanny the energy of these goddesses was and how such powers still lacked a creative outlet. The transformation of a raw energy, initially directed mainly and strictly towards the biological needs, into some kind of cultural achievement represented a great effort from human intellect that, as said above, was made possible through the advent of Christianity.

Analyzing the ceremonies above mentioned just as an outsider, one cannot help identifying the huge amount of creativity and destruction enacted there, for the Great Mothers are themselves an immense and undifferentiated power. From them everything can hatch. But then, these ceremonies were held in ritualistic character since they meant an act of reverence to such powers. However, as different cultures began to intermingle, especially during the expansion of the Roman Empire, the symbolic expression of this type of worship was somehow contaminated. There was a progressive degeneration of such practices, and a concomitant moral degradation was gradually installed as the Empire expanded its borders. What used to be *ritual* then became *literal*! The more the economy grew — the more the power relation prevailed — the greater the loss of the symbolic context. The Mediterranean cultures were then becoming progressively "Latinized" by the Roman Empire.

Obviously, the Romanization of the world brought in, primarily, an enormous diversity and cultural exchange never seen before in the history of mankind. Naturally, as part of the shadow it cast, it also caused a profound upheaval in moral and ethical values, causing an irreparable loss of group identity. Therefore, the atmosphere of the second and third centuries CE was rather fertile for the development of a new religious order which would offset the prevailing human decadence. Jung says that at the time Christianity appeared, *"spiritual values had sunk into the unconscious, and for them to surface again it would be necessary for man to take the long path of repulse against material values. Gold, women, arts, all would have to be given up."*[32]

This transitional moment in history is exemplified in the book *The Passion of Perpetua*, when Marie-Louise von Franz analyses the dreams or visions of a young Carthaginian woman from the third century CE.[33] In the book, it is possible to learn how her dreams reflected not only her inner struggles, but also the conflicts the collective was experiencing. That was a crucial moment in which the chthonic and orgiastic cults devoted to the Great Mother were being abandoned in favor of the new religious Christian creed.

Thus, as mentioned above, this newly emerging belief system overemphasized spiritual life and detachment from mundane matters. Its message starkly contrasted the way of life in course, especially concerning the idea of a better world existing in another realm, one which could only be reached through the progressive abandonment of the earthly world and all the attributes that maintain the spirit of man imprisoned in matter. All that referred to telluric existence, to matter, to flesh, went through a depreciation process and was progressively demonized.

The suppression of the feminine was greatly emphasized in this new creed. The feminine was regarded as a deity in need of substitution to the extent that its extricating represented a condition of interdiction should a human being wish to reach the "true" source of illumination and redemption in the heavenly kingdom. The feminine, therefore, being personified in women, became the incarnation of the demoniac to be avoided, repressed and controlled in this new religious order.

Hence, evil should not only be shunned but, above all, suppressed, fought against and annihilated. Achieving celestial virtue would be impossible if one had not freed himself from the

---

[32] C. G. Jung, *Analytical Psychology – Notes on the seminar given in 1925*, 68.
[33] M.-L. von Franz, *The Passion of Perpetua: A Psychological Interpretation of Her Visions*.

macula of matter. Consequently, the Christian man developed practices, attitudes and beliefs in which such an evil, and all that was associated with it, had to be expurgated. So, we can see here that there was a historically traceable shift in the religious symbolism of the Western man, which was progressively consolidated along as Christianity developed.

It must be noted, however, that everything which then escaped from man's control or could not be assimilated by him was thought to contain an archetypal diabolic character. And here we are using the most genuine meaning of the word, which comes from the Greek *diaballein*: to separate. But, even though what is diabolic is normally associated with demonic (evil), a distinction must be made between the two conditions. Any time new consciousness is conquered, that is, whenever there is differentiation from the unconscious, this is a separation, thus, diabolic. However, this may not be necessarily evil. When in the Garden of Eden, for example, Eve gave Adam the apple from the Tree of Knowledge, self-consciousness began. Then, they had to be expelled from this Paradise (a state of total unconsciousness); they were separated from the original matrix and, consequently, this may be primarily considered diabolic in the very sense of the word. In the sequence of this myth, however, such a split was qualified as demonic, evil, or a bad thing to happen. But then we may ask: for whom was it bad? Apparently, this was perceived as "bad" by the Lord (and then by His male representatives here on earth) who realized His power was not enough to control His children, both animals (the Serpent) and humans (Adam and Eve). In other words, the demonic quality is brought about mostly because Yahweh's law was not obeyed. The devilish, therefore, is what cannot be ruled by the Lord. And because it was the Serpent who whispered disobedience into Eve's ears, women were then the ones who, from then on, incorporated the demonic or evil disposition.

The paradox is the fact that the Serpent was also one of the Lord's creatures, so it was from Himself that the demonic appeared. Therefore, what may be considered demonic is the part of the Lord that He Himself could not control. But it appears that it is only after the "not controlled" thing separates that it was then named diabolic.

So, in the Judeo-Christian tradition, the pairing of the diabolic with the demonic has its origin in a power complex, while the feminine element, the woman, was its scapegoat. Nonetheless, the equating of the "demonic/evil" trait with the feminine principle is not only a prerogative of the Judeo-Christian tradition, but to trace it historically may be easier in this religious belief.

We must keep in mind, though, that the dark side of the Great Mother may be everything but *diabolic,* in the etymological sense of the word, for she has no primary interest in separating things. She is more into the assimilating mode, into eating everything up, devouring or reintegrating whatever was once created. Thus, the *diabolic* issue fits better within an analysis of the feminine from the Christian point of view. Notwithstanding, bypassing the Christian appraisal that *"the feminine is diabolic because it detours man or takes him away from his spiritualization process,"* we must not forget either to reckon and to acknowledge that the feminine has a demonic feature intrinsic to its nature as well — for the feminine, in its own right, is and must be unruly. Naturally, this is something difficult to relate to, especially for men. Such damaging and devouring features inherent to the Terrible Mother are powers which, in principle, are impossible to deal with or to "tame"; this latter being a disposition so much strived for by the masculine element. Man is always frustrated whenever he has to face the unruly, destructive side of woman: how deadly she can be, how much against life she can reveal herself to be, especially when deeply hurt. We may recall the tale of Medea, who killed her own children in order to inflict pain and regret on Jason, her betrayer-husband.

In the Hindu pantheon, we find Kali, the epitome of feminine destructiveness. But here, we know that this characteristic is something needed so that the world can always be renewed. She is included (well, she is not "included" – she just is!) in the godhead, for it takes both Kali and Shiva to bring dynamism into existence, that is, death and rebirth. According to one of the tales, in a frenzy she became so insanely ferocious and destructive that it took Shiva bowing down at her feet to calm her rage (in other versions, she realizes that she had killed Shiva only when she stumbled upon his body), and only then did she become "conscious" of her annihilating power. Psychologically, this is something the Western man is not willing to do either out of fear or pride. He is unwilling to bow to the feminine — to his soul, to his Anima — no matter how many deaths he may have to undergo in his lifetime. He will avoid it every minute and fight against that which claims for renewal inside himself, especially because it dumbfounds him.

Nevertheless, from an archetypal point of view, there is an ambivalent relationship between the masculine and the feminine principles. It is certain that the common basis is attraction, when looked upon as two extremities of the same reality. However, the intended union between these opposing poles is not always immediately able to be grasped, as one element can annihilate the other when a lack of equilibrium occurs. If such a conflict persists, the union can bear no fruit or, at the most, an anomalous fruit.

Considering man's psychology, it is certain that the feminine has always haunted or enchanted the masculine, due to its fascinating power, its irrationality, its telluric character, or for any other aspects that would be complementary or compensatory to the masculine. Such characteristics, however, cannot always be assimilated and can even become intimidating. For this reason, the masculine has a tendency to suppress or repress the feminine traits considered demonic. For a deeper dive into this topic, one might review Jung's various writings on the Anima archetype.

From the historical point of view, if the early days of Christianity could be identified as the great rebuff of the feminine, it could also be said that from the eleventh century on what occurred through the Troubadour's movement was a re-appreciation of the feminine principle. Here the feminine resurges, but underpinned by "idealization," so that the image of woman got intermingled with the image of the Virgin Mary, the ideal of perfection and purity. This Christian feminine was practically impossible to reach and, thus, became mostly an object of men's courtship. Woman turned out to be a stimulus for man to excel in his masculinity - an ideal which, unfortunately failed to build up genuine human relationships.

If from the beginning of Christianity up to the Middle Ages both woman and feminine were a pack to be disregarded, with the Troubadours one can see that man's psyche starts to break apart such perception. At this time, there was a certain condescension to a kind of virginal image of woman which, while intangible, became the target for the noblest and most altruistic sentiments of men. However, the aspect of the feminine that did not fit such an idealization was split off and demonized, eventually evolving into the figure of the witch. Thus, this latter feminine personified the object to be rejected, persecuted, and executed.

On one hand, it is possible to say that the medieval man began a "concession" to the feminine within his psychic economy, but this does not mean, at all, its integration. In his mind the feminine was still idealized, intangible, and rather celestial. It was, then, as witch that the feminine showed off the extent to which it had not been integrated and how virulent it became. The feminine as witch is that which puts man in contact with his less noble and more uncivilized feelings, more chthonic and, thus, instinctive traits. The witch represents the aspect of the feminine totality that was massacred in the beginning of the Christian era. She is the dissociated aspect of the feminine that is malefic, bewitching and rather threatening to the sentimentality of the medieval Christian.

If there was some development in the perception of the feminine with the concept of Courtly Love, its integration was still quite precarious as far as the *virginal* aspect is concerned. As witch, though, the persecution and rejection of the feminine was even more vicious; therefore, she still continues to insinuate itself hoping for redemption. It seems that woman suffers whenever she is perceived or related to under the categories of witch or of sweet dove, since what she really wants and needs is to be seen by man as human being, an earthly being, a totality.

THE FIGURE UPON WHICH EVIL IS PROJECTED IN THE FAIRYTALE

The evil woman referred to in these tales as Mooress or Saracen magnifies the assumption that the atmosphere in which such versions were created was mostly Christian. Both terms above are used for non-Christians of Islamic origin, who were strongly opposed to in the Middle Ages as they were considered heretics. We must remember that the Iberian Peninsula had been occupied by the Arabs between the eighth and fourteenth centuries CE, while the Crusades against the Muslin world began during the eleventh century CE, and the last Holy War against these people took place as late as the fifteenth century. The origin of the term Saracen, however, is somewhat more remote, being used by the Romans to refer to the North African populations, even though they were not necessarily Arabians. Later, the term was utilized to designate Islamic followers.

We can establish still another connection to the term Mooress, also observed in the Peninsula. Such a word is connected to the root *"mrvos,"* which can mean either a dead man or a supernatural man.[34] The region of Gaul has innumerous legends about the stone of the Moors, the house of the Moors, or the dolmen of the lady Moor, which are related to popular beliefs regarding megaliths built by male and female giants, both Moors. These enormous stones were considered to have great power over women's fertility.

In a Portuguese folklore book, Gallop gathers a large amount of mythological material that better illustrates the role of the lady Moor in the fantasy of the Portuguese people.[35] The expression *"enchanted Mooress"* usually refers to feminine entities who dwell in fountains, caves or mountains, and corresponds to the ancient divinities such as the Nereids or nymphs. They are associated not only with natural phenomena but also with quite primitive

---

[34] M. Alinei & F. Benozzo, Origini del Megalitismo Europeo: Un Approccio Archeo-etno-dialettologico, 295-332.
[35] R. Gallop, *Portugal - A Book of Folk Ways.*

populations which may have inhabited those lands. A Moor was also someone who had not been baptized, being therefore an individual psychologically alienated from a social and religious group.

Such enchanted Mooresses can be very beautiful, and sometimes appear with a snake's tail in place of their legs. They are only seen on the eve of Saint John, the 24th of June, when they can be observed combing their hair like the mermaids, with a golden comb. They are guardians of hidden treasures and are waiting for some human being to redeem them. In one of the tales, it is said that a young man went out to investigate an enchanted Mooress, snaked shaped, who was scaring the whole village. But during his long and tiring journey, he lay down and fell asleep. The serpent came along, kissed him and turned into a lovely maiden, and then they got married.

It is curious to note that, in the Portuguese version, it was the serpent-Mooress who kissed the young man and turned herself into a human being, not the other way round, as it is usually seen. It feels that the devilized being has some consciousness of her condition and, therefore, claims for redemption. It means that this gentleman represents the future consciousness, that is, a conscious attitude that needs to be established whenever suffering emerges due to the one-sided disposition of life. By being turned into a human being, the serpent receives acceptance into human consciousness, and this makes all the difference for the archetype — the divine, is almost always seeking to be humanized.

In the aforementioned Japanese tale ("Uriko-hime"), which is outside of the Christian culture, the figure who behaves demoniacally and replaces the melon-girl has her head cut off. That means that the way to deal with the demon is to get rid of it by cutting off its head, thereby interrupting its psychic activity. In another Japanese version, these aspects can be seen in a more impressive manner. In this version, called "The Great Melon Affair,"[36] it says:

[36] Mayer, F. H., & Kunio, Y. (1952). "Yanagita Kunio": Japanese Folk Tales. *Folklore Studies*, 11(1), i–97. https://doi.org/10.2307/1177324.

"A clairvoyant, a priest, a doctor and a warrior met at the palace of a nobleman. Some melons had been delivered as a gift, but since that was a time for fasting, the melons had to be left outside the building. The clairvoyant was asked to make a prophecy. He announced that there was poison in just one of the melons. The priest was asked to perform incantations, and after some prayers, one of the melons started to jump up and down. Then it was understood that the jumping melon was the poisoned one. So, they entreated the doctor use some needles to remove the poison. When he pierced the melon in two different spots, it stopped jumping. So, the warrior took his sword and cut open the melon in two. Everyone immediately saw that there was a small venomous snake inside the melon. The two needles had gone into its eyes, and although the warrior's sword had appeared only to cut the melon open, it actually had cut the snake's head off."

If we agree upon the fact that the snake in this culture is likewise associated with woman, this tale not only corroborates the allusion to the problem of the demoniac feminine projected on the fruit, but also displays the assembly of men trying to control their instinct of hunger. Therefore, the scenario of masculine oppression becomes complete, and the only solution is really to kill.

The association between a serpent and the feminine is further emphasized in another Japanese story called Doujoji.[37] Here, the princess feels rejected by a chaste monk who refuses her love, or else exploits it. She then transforms herself into a fiery snake that burns with jealousy. It is interesting to observe that, in both the Japanese fairytale and in this drama, the men are controlling their instincts: both their sexual drive and hunger for food. The fruit, as much as the woman, both embody the evil traits of the serpent, which are also of a tempting nature.

---

[37] S.Bérczi, O. Sano, & R. Takaki, *Snake Patterns in Eurasia/Japan and Their Implications*, 279-287.

CHAPTER 3

THE FRUIT, THE WOMAN AND THE DECAY

Fruits, in general, waste away quickly after they are harvested or cut open because of the amount of water they have inside. And the fruits referred to in these different fairytales are especially rapid in decaying. Upon interpreting the dream of Descartes in her book *A Study of the Dreams of Jung, Decartes, Socrates and Other Historical Figures*, Marie Louise Von Franz bestows certain alchemical amplifications to water as she considered the melon symbol present in the dream.[38] There she suggests that perceiving the symbolism of the fruit is instrumental in understanding the problem of the feminine/demonic because of the ease with which fruit spoils and gets rotten.

The woman, as perceived by the man, is associated with decay when menstruating. The fact that women bleed is historically considered dirty and repulsive, calling for an interdiction. Regarding her menstrual cycle, man wants to know if the woman is "pure" or "clean" enough for intercourse. In the Bible, for example, it says "*When a woman has her menstruation, she will be impure for seven days. He who touches her during this period will remain impure until sunset*" (Lev15,19). Even among the Brazilian Indian tribes, one can notice the bias against menstrual blood, since it is said that contact with it makes a man inefficient (the indigenous word is *panema*) in hunting, fishing and in other activities.

---

[38] M.-L. von Franz, *Dreams – A Study of the Dreams of Jung, Descartes, Socrates, and Other Historical Figures*.

In some cultures, menstruation was a situation for interdiction of the woman, and several restrictive rules were put down against her, such as no cooking, no leaving the house, no bathing, and so on. In recent times, pre-menstrual syndrome has been "diagnosed" as a common condition among contemporary women. A change of humor and intense irritability is associated with the syndrome, along with physical symptoms like headaches, muscular pains, swelling and other non-specific sensations. These symptoms announce through the incomprehensible — especially for the modern man — mental state that the monthly bleeding is arriving. Thus, by "diagnosing" menstruation as a syndrome, the women also interdict themselves under pre-menstrual tension. In a certain sense, then, this natural condition has also become pathologic and has been treated "preventively" by means of hormones which do not allow the menstruation to occur. This can be seen as a negation of women's nature as well. Could we say this is the biased masculine (in both woman and man) that has determined a woman's natural biological process to be a problem (transforming an organic function into a disease in need of a cure)? Or is it a self-perception of inadequacy the Animus forces on the woman? How do we balance the acquisition of conscious development with scientific developments for mitigating pain and suffering without the total substitution of the natural experience?

In some versions of the fairytale examined in the present study, the prince, having succeeded in giving water to the lady who emerged from the fruit, hastens back to his castle to get her "proper" clothing, so that she may be decently introduced to his parents and to the court. In Romero's version, there is a clear allusion to the fact that she was naked, the same happening in "The Love of The Three Pomegranates"; while in the Indian version "The Bél Princess," the prince is very tired and must rest for a while before reaching the castle. In other words, the prince needs the "persona" of the princess to be able to establish a relationship with her. Or, better said, it is necessary to wrap up what is objectionable of the feminine. Obviously, though, one cannot build up a relationship to another person, or even with the world, presenting himself or herself in the fullness of his or her own essence.

Everyone needs a certain protection, modesty or prudence when in a relationship. That is the symbolic meaning of clothing, of a psychological "persona."

From this passage, one can deduce that the prince: 1) must dress the princess suitably, 2) cannot face her nudity, or 3) has not enough energy to go on with his task. In any of these situations, it is clear that the prince is not yet prepared to deal with this new image he has just retrieved. He is either trying to fit her into his own lifestyle (by dressing her appropriately), or else he is not properly connected to his instincts to be able to fulfill his manly prerogatives. And it is at this moment of incapability, when he is unable to take hold of the share he has been endowed with, that in lurks the demon. Psychologically, this passage is extremely important because it illustrates the disaster we have to face every time we neglect the inner life, fail to deal with it in a sober manner, or just try to conform it to our own previous way. Attitudes like that are the very residence of evil.

However, the prince's intention to dress up the beautiful maiden can be understood symbolically more prospectively, as well. First, it indicates that whatever she might be, she represents something rather numinous to him. And second, exactly because such a content is numinous, one is supposed to get some protection from it; otherwise one may perish. Whenever a person starts up a dialogue with the figures belonging to the unconscious, as it happens during the technique of active imagination, it is necessary that those figures "descend" to a human level. Whenever this communication is not established on a more human level, the archetype may become more destructive than constructive. This situation is more or less illustrated by the German tale mentioned above, "The Maiden of the Waters." But it is more well-known in the mythological story of Zeus and Semele. Wanting to see Zeus in all his splendor, and ignoring his warnings, she gets burned up and perishes in the thundering magnificence of the great god.

But considering the matter from the maiden's point of view, it can be seen that being dressed is appropriate not only for the prince but also for herself. The clothing is a symbolic allusion to a mask the individual wears to present herself or himself and establish relations in social life. Such a mask constitutes the psychic function of the persona whose role in the individual's psychological dynamics is exactly that of providing some kind of protection and even a healthy distance between she/he and her/his relations. Without this protection, the individual has no differentiation, nor is she/he an *"individual"* in the more teleological sense of the expression.

At this moment of ineptitude of the masculine, the gloomy aspect of the feminine is constellated in the figure of the Crooked Mooress. Such an aspect shows itself negatively and destructively, hindering the progressive and illuminating function the Anima should work in a man's psyche.

From the point of view of the psychology of the feminine, this moment shows an immature relationship between the feminine Ego and the Animus. Such an Ego has no creative compromise and allows the opportunity for transformation to escape, sticking to convention, hence becoming a victim of its own destructive shadow. This would be a woman who avoids coming to terms with the reality of the objective psyche and fears the self-scrutiny such encounters impose on each of us.

Analyzing this theme further in the light of the psychology of woman, the Mooress/Saracen/Negress is, at the most, a characterization of the constellation of the maiden's shadow, as mentioned before. But it is interesting to observe how the shadow acts in this plot. In a suitable situation, she shows up and wants to take over the place of the maiden. Anytime an archetypal material fails to be acknowledged by consciousness it has a bewitching effect, and that is what happens to this shadowy feminine content; that is, it mesmerizes the Ego and overcomes it.

Three times does the black woman break the ceramic jar used for fetching water, and three times she is reprimanded by her mistress, who orders her back to finish her task. Jars and bowls are manmade household utensils which were created alongside important cultural developments, allowing the storage of victuals in different communities across the globe. They are typically feminine, both in their making and in their shape, especially because in various ancient cultures they were more often made by women. In a certain sense, when a woman first manufactured clay pots, she was reproducing, externally, an inner experience. The pot is like her uterus that holds and nurtures that which is developing. According to Marie-Louise von Franz, such earthenware represents, in some way, a feminine mystery that leads us to Anael, the demoniac angel from the old alchemical text *"Isis to Horus."* He appears as a *semeion* (sign or symbol), carrying a vase with the secret alchemical substance Isis is searching for.[39] So, in the fairytale, when the Mooress breaks the jar three times, she, in a sense, abdicates from the feminine mystery (Could we see here the roots for the pre-menstrual "syndrome" treatment?). Eros, in his more civilized fashion, has been renounced, and his destructive, obsessive and possessive sides have become more active. The Saracen with the broken jar represents the unleashed shadow of Eros — the power complex.

As discussed previously, we could see that the feminine being considered both diabolic and demonic under the Judeo-Christian tradition was a function of the constellation of a power complex in man or in whatever personifies the masculine principle. The activation of the power complex means that a relationship based on feelings is hampered or even inexistent. However, as it can be seen by our group of fairytales, such a hindering occurs not only in men, but in women as well. Abdicating from Eros in its differentiated aspect, as allegorically represented by the breaking of the jar, the Mooress reveals how invested in power she is. The shadow of Eros is power, and that is what degrades any relationship because under this condition, there is only Ego playing out between the pair of supposed "lovers" — a real and genuine feeling anchored in the Self is gone! Therefore, instead of a progression towards higher consciousness, what we see instead is a gradual reabsorption of the elements by the unconscious. Now, the beautiful maiden regresses into an animal form.

---

[39] M.-L. von Franz, *A Paixao de Perpetua: Uma Interpretacao Psicologica de Suas Visoes,* Ed. Privada.

The shadow, in Jungian language, is that psychic function mostly related to the unconscious, for it carries what is unknown and not admitted by consciousness. But once it is constellated, the shadow always causes a negative impression on the Ego because it perceives, through projection, everything that is rejected, frightening and out of reach, but which belongs, indeed, to the Ego itself. In this manner, the shadow assails the Ego whenever the latter is not aware of what has been alienated from itself. Of course, there is also the positive shadow, which carries prospective contents we do not recognize in ourselves, but this does not seem to be the case in this version.

In the tales, there is the figure of the "mistress" of this Mooress, who insists that she must go back to accomplish her unfinished task. This leads us to believe that the mistress is a figure in service of the Self, as her task in the plot is to make the Crooked Mooress — the shadow "function" — fulfill its destiny. One of the prerogatives of the Self is to unite the opposites, to make possible a certain balance between the inner forces that tend to tear apart the individual. It is not by chance that, similar to the princess who needed water to come out of the fruit, it is the very shadow of the princess that carries that water every day. That is, both the princess and the mistress need water. Psychologically speaking, this finding is widely known in Jungian practice, for it is in the shadow, in the rejected contents, that the elixir of life can be found. Hence, the Self practically foists contents upon the Ego so that they may be assimilated. Following this rationale, the Mooress/Saracen/Negress is an aspect of the woman's psyche that bids for redemption from within and will continue to assert itself until it is assimilated, or else it will be the Ego who will lose itself in its own shadow.

On the other hand, the role of the Mooress in these tales performs a more important function for the figure of the prince, for she represents an aspect of the negative feminine which he must learn to deal with. We could say that, for that man, the Negress is an aspect of his Anima that appears demonized and, thus, usurping. But she also lends completeness to the feminine. In other words, man must learn how to relate both to women and to his Anima, considering them in their totality, not only their angelical, tamed, submissive countenances. If man fails to approach the not-yet-illuminated aspect of his soul (or of "his" woman) he himself falls victim of black magic and bewitchment as well. The container for his creativity is broken!

But it is possible to continue analyzing this theme from the woman's point of view, considering another disposition of the psychic functions. This is important to be mentioned because the fairytale should not be interpreted only from the masculine point of view nor uniquely from the feminine's. Actually, such tales have to do with the interaction of the characters within the unconscious and, as such, common to both man and woman.

So, if we take the prince as a pre-figuration of the Animus, the maiden as the "ego,"[40] and the destructive aspect of the Mooress/Saracen, impersonated now as the figure of the Great Mother, or the negative maternal complex, we will then have a proper scenario illustrating the hardship women go through in their process of inner growth. Up to now, we have emphasized that the feminine entrapped in the fruit was mostly related to the disastrous relationship established with the masculine principle. That is to say her refuge in the fruits was a consequence of her experiences with the masculine. But the fact is that the Great Mother, or the negative maternal complex, harbors a mortal "envy" of the newly-arriving feminine. In the myth "Amor and Psyche," in "Snow White and the Seven Dwarfs", or in "Cinderella," this harmful and envious aspect of the Great Mother is quite well depicted. Whenever a woman is entrapped within a fruit by a negative mother complex, it can also be said that she is being incarcerated within what has not been consciously or properly lived by her feminine principle. As a friend female Jungian analyst once commented with me, such a woman "identifies herself with the juicy and savoriness of life, the tastiness and beauty of the sensual side of life, and with the colorful art of enticement, but

---

[40] "Ego" is under quotation because all these characters belong to the collective unconscious and, therefore, one cannot talk about a real ego. Thus, it is as if we were saying: "if we identify the figure of the princess as an ego..."

everything is still unconscious," somehow autonomous. And as long as a woman is unconsciously identified with these values inside the fruit, she only plays the luring aspect of the Anima for men. It seems that it takes a robust man or a good Animus figure to rescue the feminine from the fruit, to severe such an unconscious identification. But as we could learn from the story, the masculine principle did only half and, in certain ways, a lousy job, for the negative mother complex took over again. The stealing of the princess' place by the Saracen, and her subsequent transformation into a flying creature, points to the annihilating power of the maternal complex over the psychic development of the daughter. Women who experience the feminine archetype in a negative way are only capable of creative realization when there is a prolific experience with the positive Animus or a real Man. Actually, a woman who is identified with a too luring "eros" capacity is rather unconscious.

The way the black woman puts the princess down is by means of a needle-pricking. This motif will be discussed later, but, for now, what can be seen regarding a woman with a negative maternal complex is actually a standstill in her development which makes her incapable of opening up to a typical feminine life.

THE REVIVIFYING QUALITY OF THE FRUIT

Coming back to the fruits, not only watermelons, but orange, lemons, citrons, quinces, melons, and most especially pome-granates, all have a large amount of seeds. Thus, the association with fertility is inevitable. If we examine the different versions of the tales, we find that all the fruit mentioned belong to the Magnoliophyta division, also called angiosperm ("hidden seed"). These plants have in common the fact that the ovule develops inside a seed hidden in the ovary which is the fruit itself. Hence, from a symbolic view, the fact that a beautiful lady emerges from this fruit seems to be an obvious allusion to the assumption that the power for fructification and continuity of life must be retrieved from its enclosure. It is from within the "fruit" that man will get refreshment for his dull life, whence he will again get some vitality and purpose for living. Psychologically speaking, it turns out to be a challenging task because the feminine principle, set aside through suppression or repression, becomes hurt, wounded, resentful and angry. It also tends to antagonize and eventually becomes revengeful towards the masculine principle, in a rather demonic fashion. But, by cutting through the fruit, our gentleman embraces this complicated situation; he takes up the problem of the Anima and accepts the conflict between good and evil. Thus, this may be the most appropriate way by which his consciousness can be lifted up because only through that action life, then, has been tried out.

It is interesting to note that this symbolism has an archetypal quality, occurring in dreams not only of men but also of women with a conspicuous Animus and blatant Logos, as can be found these days. Its compensating feature, however, can only be understood in the context of the dreamer and his or her own associations. Below is the dream of a man under analysis where this symbolism can be seen:

"I am on the top of a wall and my father is angrily throwing oranges at me, trying to hit me as if I were a target."

Concerning the associations, the dreamer says he lived in a household whose structure was deeply feminine, and his father, who had already passed away by the time of this dream, had a lifelong story of alcohol abuse. At present, he is married, but his wife is having difficulties in becoming pregnant; even when she does conceive, she has had spontaneous abortions. During a great part of his life, including the time he lived with his parents, the dreamer used to have erotic fantasies about the Virgin Mary, so he developed a practice of fervent prayer in order to expiate such sinful thoughts "instilled by the devil" [*sic*]. He also developed ritualistic and obsessive hygienic behavior, for fear that his mother or sisters should become pregnant from the semen resulting from his compulsive masturbating activity. In the dream, he is surprised by the violence with which his father hurls the oranges at him, in contrast to the lovingly peeled oranges his mother usually serves him in everyday life.

This dream along with its associations illustrates quite well the issue under discussion involving the problem of the masculine depotentiation and his neurotic behavior (*being on the top of the wall*) and obsessive/compulsive symptoms (prayers, excessive hygiene and uncontrolled masturbation) as a means of "draining off" the libido, so far directed in a wrong way. His life is marked by a disruption of instincts, which is typical of the Christian faith, as well as the demonization of the feminine.

The neurotic incarceration is revealed by the desire to fulfill the instinctual urge — the sexual drive — with the feminine figure, which in this case, is portrayed as the utmost in spirituality and non-tangential materiality, the Virgin Mary. Satisfying the instincts is not only forbidden, but also sinful! Hence, the Virgin and the diabolic become autonomous contents in the psyche of this dreamer, resulting in the obsessive symptoms of different nuances.

The feminine in the psyche of this dreamer becomes idealized, as with the Troubadours, in the figure of the Virgin. But even so, the connection of this feminine with its chthonic, and therefore dark roots, is still rather alive in the dreamer through his uncontrolled instinctive sexual impulses. In other words, the feminine in the psychic economy of this man is shattered. In a compensating manner, then, the unconscious imposes upon the dreamer an irresistible desire for sexual union with Mary.

It is interesting to point out that, through the desire to have an intercourse with Mary, this man's unconscious reveals his need to engender his own image of Christ. This means that the solution to his conflict requires him to father a redemption symbol — a symbol of union and reconciliation of the opposites — just like the one who was miraculously born from the Virgin Mary. But both the divine figures of Mary and Christ are symbols that need to be realized in mundane life, be it through relations with people or displaying a more robust and sound way of living.

Considering that the Virgin Mary is the mother of all of us, the fantasy of this dreamer leads us to the idea of incest, more so because he is "afraid" that his real mother and sisters may become pregnant from his ejaculated semen. However, as suggested by Jung, such incest is not intended simply as cohabitation with his mother, but shows a special kind of nostalgia to become an infant again, that is, a need to renew himself. [41] This is very much akin to the old Egyptian motif of "kamutef," "*the bull of his mother*," a designation of Osiris who, by having intercourse with Isis, is newly begotten from his wife/mother. Actually, it is a desire to return to parental protection, to return to his mother to be born again, revivified.

In the above case, the masculine principle who was supposed to direct the dreamer in life is "anesthetized": his father was an alcoholic. He does not manage to fertilize his wife (or the fertilization never comes to term), while his incestuous and sinful fantasies reflect the demonized condition he is experiencing. It should be noted, however, that it is still the masculine principle, represented in the dream by his "father" who shows affect and energy, even though in a negative manner. It is he who reacts with some anger, thus demonstrating emotional life when throwing the oranges at him. There is, then, some sort of intention in the psyche of this dreamer to be understood, still concealed in the oranges. But through studies of comparative material, it might be possible to gather some clues about it.

It is quite likely that the dreamer should have to take care of the oranges thrown at him by his father. It must be noted that whenever one is eating round fruits or playing with spherical objects, it is symbolically an expression of wholeness. He actually should get the means to heal the problem of the feminine split in his soul, which is the whole problem of love. The Virgin Mary is a kind of insubstantial feminine, as untouchable as the feminine inside the oranges of this dreamer! The difference is that, with the latter, the chances for union may be possible through the confrontation with the masculine energy numbed inside himself.

The association between citric fruit and the feminine can also be found in ancient traditions, for a lemon tree was always planted in the center of nearly all the small villages or towns of Germany.

---

[41] C. G. Jung, *Symbols of Transformation*, CW 5, §351.

According to Marie-Louise von Franz, it was a feminine symbol dedicated to the divine nature of goddesses like Perchta, Hulda and Holle, besides others. It was believed that the souls of unborn children dwelt under the leaves of those trees. Such trees were like a central axis for the community, the same way the American Indians enacted their ritual practices around trees.[42] In the Far East, oranges were often offered to young ladies when proposing marriage since these fruits bring good fortune and immortality because they come from eternal trees.

But it is also significant to mention that oranges can also be used for black magic. In the old British folk tale, it was said that whenever one wanted to destroy a person, one should write his or her name on a piece of paper which was afterwards pushed into an orange. Then, this fruit was placed at the top of a chimney until the person dies.[43] Such a superstition illustrates quite well that the entrapment of the feminine within the oranges in these fairytales could be more than a simple repression or suppression. It could really mean annihilation!

Men with an exaggerated positive maternal complex are often jeopardized in the development of their masculinity and instinctual life. It is not uncommon that such men may eventually cultivate a rather one-sided intellectual lifestyle in order to counterbalance the maternal energy. A bright intellect acts as an antidote or a protection against the all-encompassing and amalgamating tendency of the motherliness of the feminine. But, sooner or later, these men must face up to their overbearing feminine for the sake of their psychic totality. The demon, in this situation (and others as well), acts as the *"principium individuationis."*

In the same way as in the dream above, we can observe a more subtle example of the modernity of this fruit-image through the Word Association Test. Here, the client in question is a married adult man, who lost his father while still a child. He shows a strong

---

[42] M.-L. von Franz, *Puer Aeternus: A Psychological Study of the Adult Struggle with the Paradise of Childhood*, 196.
[43] A. Maguire, *Skin Disease – A Message from the Soul: A Treatise from a Jungian Perspective of Psychosomatic Dermatology*, 90.

positive mother complex, and in his professional life, he performs activities which require deep intellectual and literary devotion. During the test, the stimulating word loquat (medlar) caused the longest lapse of time before an answer. After analyzing the test and talking it over with the client, it became evident that his neurotic problem is linked to the intense presence of his mother and his deviation from instinctive life. But it was not clear to him why he took such a long time to make an association with the "loquat" or why this fruit represented a complex for him. The fact was that he was going through a serious crisis with his wife, a woman of Asian descent, the very region where the loquat is supposed to originally come from (the scientific name of this fruit is *Eriobotrya japonica*).

So, the contents of the complex activated by that stimulus, that is, his dealings with the feminine, were deeply buried in the unconscious, even though he recognized, intellectually, the strong pull his mother had in his life and acknowledged the conflict in his marriage. In other words, there is this claiming of an Anima whose characteristics appear to be more chthonic, less ethereal and more embodied, insinuating herself to this young man, as revealed by the association word test.

The loquat is a fruit said to rot before it gets ripe, thus is represented figuratively in the literature as a symbol for prostitution and premature decay. In British literature, the loquat has as strong sexual connotation associated with the desired feminine, in its carnal and instinctual aspects. In Romeo and Juliet, Shakespeare makes use of this fruit to point out such a characteristic when Mercutio laughs at Romeo's disquieted love for his mistress Rosaline (Act II, 1, 34-38):

> "If love be blind, love cannot hit the mark.
> Now will he sit under a medlar tree,
> And wish his mistress were that kind of fruit
> As maids call medlars, when they laugh alone.
> Romeo, that she were, O, that she were
> An open **open-arse**, thou a **pop'rin pear**!

Romeo, good night: I'll to my truckle-bed;
This field-bed is too cold for me to sleep:
Come, shall we go?"

In this fragment of Shakespeare's play, the expression "open-arse," the vulgar connotation of medlar, is usually omitted and substituted by "et cetera." The fruit meant by *open-arse* is an allusion to its form which emulates the female genitalia.[44] In the same sense, the word *"pop'rin pear"* is an euphemism for penis, rather common in the British literature of sixteenth century because of the association between this fruit and the erect penis and scrotum. But it was also used as a pun for copulation since "pop in" means to thrust, to penetrate.

However, considering that this image of the entrapped feminine within fruit is an archetypical question, it should not be restricted to a specific gender, for, as said, a woman with a rather destructive negative mother complex has her development seriously hampered. We have observed the same issue in a middle-aged woman under Jungian analysis. One of the main reasons that brought her to therapy was a rather one-sided development of the Animus which led to a hypertrophy of the Logos and a strong rationality that sterilized her Eros life, either as a wife, mother, daughter or friend. She had been somewhat aloof, extremely dedicated to her work and having an almost military domestic routine. This client brought in the following dream:

"...I was going down a hill and saw a mango tree with no leaves. There were only the fruits; very yellow and ripe, looking very tasty. I asked my husband to pick some for me, but the lady who owned the tree appeared. She was an old woman who said to me: '- If you want these fruits, you'll have to buy them!'"

---

[44] M. Delahoyde, http://public.wsu.edu/~delahoyd/shakespeare/r&j2.html, November 2012.

The fact that this woman was going down, and not up the hill, suggests a necessity of departure from the heights, the domain of ideas and Logos. It seems to be time to approach the earth, the telluric essence, which is the feminine realm. However, on the way down, she finds a tree with no leaves. In a general sense, a tree is a pervasive symbol of the feminine, for, among the several possibilities of interpretation, it is what has the capability to create its fruits anew. But this tree is shown in a paradoxical manner; on one side, it lacks life (no leaves), but on the other, it is full of life and nutrition (bearing ripe fruits). In a different fairytale, we can find the situation where a future event is associated with something sprouting from a tree.[45]

We can see in this case that the nourishment the woman longs for, obtainable with the help of her husband (help from the positive Animus which quite often is close to Eros), belongs to the archetypical figure of the Great Mother. But she cannot account only on the help from her husband, as an "instrument," to get the fruit. She must pay for them; that is, she has to offer psychic energy in order to gain such nutrition. A woman with a negative mother complex is often under possessed by the negative Animus and becomes cut off from her erotic capacity. The leafless tree may be an allusion to the dryness the woman experiences resulting from her submission to an oppressive Animus. Eros, like the mangos, is retained under the deeper powers of the unconscious (the old woman), who only delivers the treasure when an energy of the same intensity is given back in return. So, here we have the old motif of the young lady having to work hard under the tyranny of the negative Great Mother (witch).

The tree in this dream, however, appears paradoxical, for it is half-dead but is also in the full act of giving. In the Tarot, there is a card called the Hanged Man. It is usually represented with a man hanging himself from a tree with no leaves. This can be understood as a metaphor for the man who is not living a normal life on earth, but a dreamy, idealistic life.[46] This may also refer to the situation

---

[45] C. G. Jung, *Symbols of Transformation* CW 5, §367.
[46] J.E. Cirlot, *A Dictionary of Symbols*, second edition.

of the woman dreamer due to the sterile condition brought about by her Animus and Logos. But this same image also indicates that her erotic capacity can still be restored. It is necessary, therefore, to make a psychic investment for this to happen. So, this dream points to the same problem of the feminine/Eros element being hanged on a tree, as in our group of fairytales, but concerns the difficulties of modern women connecting to their own essence.

In a certain sense, this woman's dream supports her investment in the analytical process as far as the search for her own essence is concerned. As she enhances her self-knowledge, she also becomes more receptive to a new form of the feminine which is coming closer to her and offers itself to her. But the dreamer must work in order to be worthy of enjoying it. Eros, with the help of the husband, has the possibility of being rescued, for it is basically through relationships between man and woman — through the erotic capacity and bonding — that life may flow back again. But, once more, it is necessary that this woman invests libido in it, so that the negativity of the mother complex may be transformed.

Now, the mangos, from a psychological point of view, have the same meaning for the Hindus as the apples have for us Westerners. Symbolically they are linked to feelings, either of love when concerning the goddesses or to knowledge when the figure of Ganesh, the Elephant God, is present. A legend is told that the god Indra, learning that there was a mango tree with an enormous fruit which nobody could manage to pick up, descends to Earth and harvests the fruit. But a drop of white sap from the branch he broke doing so falls into one of his three eyes, causing it to become blind. He then throws away the mango, and from inside it appears a princess.[47] The psychological meaning of this legend indicates that, for the feminine to flourish in the masculine, it requires some sacrifice of the capacity to see what is in the outside world in favor of an inward look into the internal world. To relate properly to a woman, man must come to terms with his feminine soul – the

[47] A. Ratnasinghe, http://www.angelfire.com/planet/heritagesl2/nawagamuwa/nawa gamuwa2.htm. Last access Dec. 2010.

Anima. Indra now sees the collective with only two eyes, while with the blind eye he sees inside himself. Therefore, once a man becomes conscious of his Anima, there is no way to avoid a permanent inner scrutiny as far as the subjective life is concerned.

This mysterious archetypal display involving the mango fruit and the feminine can still be appreciated in a dream of a man under analysis. He dreamed he was under a tree that bore huge mango fruits. They looked like enormous breasts, ready to fall on him. He was somehow preoccupied with the outcome, although it appeared to be a correct thing to happen, for nobody else was concerned. This dream suggested that this was the ripe moment for him to face the dealings with the anima. He commented that it was, indeed, an image of life, of abundance.

A woman, also in analysis, has the following dream: she dreams that her female friend hurls lemons at the analysand's husband because she dislikes his painting (in the dream it was the husband who painted, not the dreamer herself). The dreamer is actually a painter, but even though she is creative, she lacks eros and feeling in her relationships. The dreamer's friend represents her shadow aspect for she is very considerate about other people and caring in her relationships. By throwing lemons at the dreamer's husband, she conveys that the dreamer's Animus may be creative, but it lacks Eros or something which favor the feminine principle. In a way, she wants him to be somehow juicier.

The fact that the versions of the fairytales refer to distinct fruits may indicate that different aspects are meant by each of them. The variation in the use of the fruits may also be taken up according to the geographic area where a certain type of fruit may be more abundant than others. Anyway, it is worth trying to understand some of them from a symbolic point of view. In any event though, as mentioned before, all these fruits are associated with fertility, just as water is to the feminine. In the following paragraphs, some of the fruits referred to in the fairytale are discussed based on their probable psychological meaning.

Both the melon and the watermelon, which belong to the same family, *cucurbitaceous*, have a great amount of water and seeds and are not always easy to digest. It is worth mentioning that the expression *"cucurbitae"* refers to the alchemical vase, retort, where the transforming processes occur. In the I-Ching, (hexagram 44), it says that the melon is a symbol for the beginning of darkness and, although sweet to taste, deteriorates quite rapidly. Thus, it belongs to the Yin principle, which is feminine.[48]

The hexagram above mentioned talks of a ripe melon that falls from the sky at the exact moment that the powers of heaven and earth meet one another and *"all things are unveiled in their maximum material capacity, where obscure forces no longer disturb the powers of light."* This means the melon contains a natural order which, at the right moment **can** "fall" without causing any harm. As Marie-Louise von Franz asserts, the melon *"represents a latent order within the dark which may be suddenly and unexpectedly revealed"* and appears *"as an obscure hetaeristic image of the Anima, but also bearing a portion of non-assimilating and non-adulterated nature that is dangerous to the conventional human order."* She also mentions that melons were the food so much appreciated and missed by some renitent Hebrew followers who joined Moses while escaping from Egypt; thus, it represents the nourishment of the heretic shadow of the Jews and Christians.[49]

The correlation between fruits rich in seeds, the feminine and the dark side of existence can be observed amongst the Manichean Gnostics, as observed by Marie-Louise von Franz: *"their system of belief was dualistic, in which God was represented by light and spirit, while Satan was associated to darkness and to the material world. The human beings, created by God, were divine spirits who fell upon the Earth, where they started carrying inside themselves the seeds of darkness, sowed by Satan, because of their material bodies. Thence, the aim of this religion was to liberate the soul and the light imprisoned in the bodily darkness by means of ascetic practices. Due to the rejection of matter, the Manicheans considered evil as being more a physical than a moral question. Women, then, were looked on as gloomy forces, once they had*

---

[48] M.-L. von Franz, *Dreams – A Study of the Dreams of Jung, Descartes, Socrates, and Other Historical Figures.*
[49] *Ibid.*

power to attract men to the mundane pleasures, keeping them away from their spiritual quest."

One of the rites among the practitioners of this religion was to ingest fruits with a large amount of seeds, such as cucumber and especially melon, for they were believed to contain great quantities of Light waiting to be redeemed from imprisonment in the material aspect of the fruit. The idea was that such individuals — the elected ones living a pure ascetic life — would be able to *"'preserve' the seeds of light, so that when they died, they could return them to their existence in the divine kingdom again. The melon, for its roundness and its bright yellow color, acted as a convenient hook for the projection of the divine/solar light of the practitioner."*[50]

Jung commented that one of the aspects of the sun in alchemy is related to an active substance hidden in the gold which can be extracted as *tinctura rubea*. This active solar substance means that the alchemical Sol is more a *"virtus (Latin: corporeal force), a mysterious power with regenerative and transformative character... And as a balsam, its substance drips from the sun and produces lemons, oranges, wine and, in the mineral kingdom, gold."*[51]

The same vivifying feature of the fruits can also be observed through the extraction of their juice, and this aspect is taken up in different manners according to different cultures. The term *Chymia*, for example, associated to the origin of the word "alchemy," is primarily related to the production of juice used in drugs, magic potions and other procedures that are supposed to bring transformation to the human body. Chymia is of Egyptian origin and is associated with the verb *km*, which means to complete, to finish, to perform (the preparation of the balms) and to conclude (the metallurgic work). And so, *km*, in a certain sense, refers to the repetition of the original creation of the world and is also associated with the extraction of juice.[52]

---

[50] *Ibid.*
[51] C. G. Jung, *Mysterium Coniunctionis* CW 14, §110 ff.
[52] J. Lindsay, *The Origins of Alchemy in Graeco-Roman Egypt*, 74.

In Greek, though, the word "alchemy" (Arab *'al'* = the and Greek *'χυμός'* = *kumos* = *chymeia*) means juice, properly, the restoring liquid. So, *"the juice would represent the quintessential quality of the work which, here, in the context of the fairytale, is related to the love-experience. It is a god-like substance, the Anima, that man should extract, for such an experience is what bestows eternal life and sets free that which is under a state of obsession."*[53]

In the book *Transforming Sexuality*, Ulanov and Ulanov report the dream of a young man who lived under the extreme influence of a powerful mother complex. He also achieved a high degree of development of his intellect as an antidote to the castrating Animus of his mother (as pointed out above). Naturally, the instincts of this young man were either paralyzed or restrained when he was in the vicinity of his mother. In the dream, he receives a large can of frozen orange juice. As he warms it up and melts its contents, an infant appears right in the middle of it, in an almost embryonic stage, but alive and breathing.[54]

The motif of being reborn through the extraction of juice from a fruit is quite ancient and can be seen engraved on a tomb dated from 550-530 BCE, in Lakonia (figure). It depicts a couple, in the form of divine beings or heroes, with the man holding a large jar while squeezing juice through a long piece of cloth.[55] The juice is coming from a pomegranate the woman holds, as she helps

---

[53] R.B. Onias, *The Origins of European Thought – About the Body, the Mind, the Soul, the World, Time and Fat*, 281 (notes).

[54] A. Ulanov & B. Ulanov, *Transforming Sexuality The Archetypal World of Anima and Animus*, 71.

[55] G. Salapata, "The Tippling Serpent in the Art of Lakonia and Beyond." Hesperia: The Journal of the American School of Classical Studies at Athens 75, no. 4 (2006): 541–60. https://www.jstor.org/stable/i25067997.

with the procedure. Below, in front of the throne, there is a boy holding a cock and an egg, and a girl with a lotus (or pomegranate?) flower, and a pomegranate. This relief is clearly a representation of rebirth through the fruit juice.

Actually, it seems that pomegranates were not primarily associated with fertility, as it was later discovered in modern Greece, but really with resurrection. In the Kabeiroi Mysteries, the ingestion of pomegranates was forbidden, as their seeds were believed to come from the tree that grew from the blood of Dionysus after he was slain and left on the ground. Other legends have it that a pomegranate tree sprouted from the tomb of Menoikeus, who killed himself at the entry door of Thebes in order to save the town. According to Pausanias: *"if you cut open the pomegranate from the tree which sprouted from the tomb of Menoikeus, you will see there is blood inside it..."*

We have still another connection between the pomegranate and the death of Attis. Again, those initiated in the mysteries of Cybele and Attis were forbidden to eat the fruit, meanwhile the priests carried them in their hands or wore wreaths made of them. Nana (another name for the Great Goddess) ate a pomegranate and conceived Attis; then the fruit became a pledge to the immortality of the initiated ones. Thus, the prohibition of eating those fruit is due to fear that *"the soul should take over the body."* In modern psychology, we could understand this as the danger of a man being possessed by the Anima and losing his masculinity by becoming too sentimental or even effeminate, for that is what threatens a boy with an overwhelming positive mother complex.

In a way, then, it is possible to identify the pomegranate as a fruit with magic properties, dating back to the Kabeiroi Mysteries. There, the fruit was used in rituals of birth and death, and was also considered auspicious during critical moments of change (initiation), especially under the tutelage of the Great Mother. It is interesting to see that in several Portuguese paintings of the sixteenth century, artists like Gregorio Lopes and Cristóvão de Figueiredo depict pomegranates, linen cloth and the juice from the fruit on the deathbed of figures associated with the Catholic pantheon, leading us to the idea of resurrection.

Of course, fertility is the most frequent association to the fruit due to its abundance of seeds. In the same way, melons, watermelons and oranges, among others, have that appeal. In Vietnam, for example, it is customary to offer a young couple seeds from melons and oranges.[56] In the myth of Persephone, we find the most widely known connection between this fruit and fertility. When she ate the pomegranates in the kingdom of Hades, she integrated the chthonic feminine she was shielded from in the upper world. Thus, the mystery of fertility was incorporated in Persephone.

In Christian imagery, the pomegranate is considered to be the fruit of conformity, harmony and union, as the seeds are harmoniously united inside it. Hence, it became for the Catholic Church a symbol of union and faith.[57] And the Bible says that the cheeks of the wife are like the two halves of the pomegranate (Songs 4, 3) — the expression of love.

In the Sílvio Romero's version, however, the fruit which appears is the watermelon. It is impossible to separate this version from its Iberian influence, as it is worth saying that this fruit was first introduced when the Moors were still in Europe, around the thirteenth century CE.[58] Nevertheless, associations with the watermelon follow the same lines as the other fruits mentioned above. There are, for example, reports of watermelon seeds being deposited in the tombs of the pharaohs of ancient Egypt more than five thousand years ago, as one means of sustaining life after death. It has been reported that among a group of Amerindians in South American, a person who dreams of a melon will encounter a cadaver. Also, it is said that the souls of the deceased, while undergoing all trials before redemption, are given meat in the

[56] J. Chevalier & A. Gheerbrant, *Dictionary of Symbols*.
[57] I. de Barreira, *Tratado das significaçoens das plantas, flores, e fruttos, que se referem na Sagrada Escrittura : tiradas de divinas, e humanas letras, com suas breves considerações / pelo Padre Fr. Isidoro de Barreyra. 1634, p. 136.* http://objdigital. bn.br/acervo_digital/div_obrasraras/or_21_4_17/or_21_4_17_item1/index.html. Last access Oct. 2021.
[58] J.F. Mariani, *The Dictionary of American Food and Drink*.

shape of melons, to certify whether it is capable of live among the dead.[59]

The Persians used to travel through the Alborz Mountains, for they believed that Mithra had been born from the light coming from the caves existing there. The festival to celebrate his birth is called Shab-e Yalda and takes place on the 21st of December. To this day, Iranians gather to read poetry and to eat and drink on this date, when both the pomegranate and the watermelon have a special meaning, for their red color symbolizes the red seen at daybreak and the glimmer of life that relates to the splendor of Mithra. And as the Shab-e Yalda happens during the winter solstice — the longest night of the year — its symbolism in Persian poetry is associated with separation from a loved one; loneliness and waiting; and, consequently, with celebrating a reunion when the night is over. Here it is evident that celebrating Mithra has to do with the Sun rising every day, so Light and Good overcome Darkness and Evil.

During these celebrations, the oldest member of the family says prayers, giving thanks to God for the past year and asking for prosperity during the year to come. He then cuts a melon or a watermelon and gives a piece to everyone who is present. Cutting represents the extirpation of sickness and pain in the family, while the ingestion of the fruit, together with walnuts, pomegranates and seeds (mainly of watermelon and marrows) meant prosperity in days to come. Thus, in an analogous manner to the fairytales discussed here, the celebrant extracts from the fruit that which remediates!

Now the quince, another fruit commonly found in fairytales, is associated with commitment between couples. In Greece, it was customary for women to rub pieces of this fruit on their lips, so they would be perfumed just before entering the marital chamber. In the fairytale "The Bél Princess," the word "bél" (bel-tree) refers to the quince, whose scientific name is *Aegle marmelos*. Aegle in Greek mythology is the name of one of Asclepius' daughters. This name means "shine" and "splendor," which comes from the beauty of a healthy body or else refers to the tributes paid to the medical

---

[59] J. Wilbert, *Puertas del Averno*. Sociedad de Ciencias Naturales la Salle, p. 161-175.

profession. She was also an assistant to her father, this great physician of the Greek world.[60] In this sense, in the fairytale featuring the quince, its regenerating and conciliatory aspects are highlighted.

In Ruth Guimarães' version ("The Little Dove and The Crooked Mooress"), when the god-son received the three quinces from the fairy, he somehow regretted it for he states: "*this fruit may not be sucked because its juice is sour.*" This remark must not go unnoticed, for such a sourness is also found with lemons and ciders; fruits which are also mentioned in other versions. What we could learn from the bitterness of these fruits is that dealing with the Anima is not just a "mellow" endeavor. It is not always a "*prêt-à-porter*" kind of business. To attempt to have a whole and fulfilling relationship with a woman or to come to terms with the Anima when one carries a bias about the feminine being innocent or kind virgins just waiting to be savored is a very naïve, if not a troubadouristic assumption. Engaging with the feminine, either in the form of a real woman or as a psychic function such as the Anima, presupposes the fact they are also bitter, thorny, not sweet, and often times hard to swallow.

Generally speaking, what all these fairytales have in common is the fact that the feminine element was somehow preserved inside a certain kind of fruit, waiting for redemption. But one must recall that each fruit utilized in a given tale may have its own specific implication, as explored above.

Returning to the male dreamer along with the individual who completed the word association test mentioned before, one cannot help but reflect on the symbolic meaning inherent in the fruits. The amplification of the fruits which was carried out in the context of these fairytales enabled us to expand our understanding of their possible meaning. It does not seem improbable then, that the fruit in the dream and in the word association test could lead to crucial questions related to the feminine in the psychic economy of each one, that is, the love problem.

---

[60] In http://www.theoi.com/Ouranios/AsklepiasAigle.html. Last access April 2010.

CHAPTER 4

THE TRANSFORMATION OF THE MAIDEN

Continuing with the narratives, it can be observed that the Mooress/Saracen/Negress, upon discovering the maiden, lures her to a trap that will cause this newly arisen feminine to be obfuscated. The new disappearance of that which would be a more prospective feminine figure, so to speak, coincides with its counterpart taking an action. At this moment, the feminine with gloomy, regressive and destructive characteristics will assume the role of the leading actress in the plot. This is an important psychological condition, for it illustrates the fact that, each and any content, when it becomes conscious but is not properly accommodated by the Ego, tends to sink back again into the unconscious, as mentioned before.

In several versions, the way the Mooress subverts the maiden is by pretending she would help the young lady with her hair that she might appear more attractive to the prince. First, it is important to note that hair is a tegument that grows from the head. Hence, it is symbolically associated with thoughts and ideas, which also "spring" from the head, one could say. In dreams, hair grooming activities could be a symbolic expression of issues related to thoughts and ideas. Washing, cutting, dyeing, disentangling and combing the hair can be understood as representations for the need to clean, to adjust, to give a different view, to sort out or to straighten up thoughts and ideas and so forth.

Secondly, the maiden obviously "falls" in the trap set by the Mooress, who, being a woman, also understands the weakness of the feminine revealed through cosmetic vanity. The cosmetic industry, fashion and accessories are in general mostly directed to the feminine public, offering a larger choice of products than what is made available for the male public. But men, of course, can also get immolated in the fire of vanities, including favoring cosmetics, for the Anima in men in modern times is much less censored as compared to former times. Nonetheless, the Anima still instills illusions on them, since one of the latest fashions among men is to implant silicone prosthesis to give them a more manly appearance and a sense of virility. Barbara Hannah says that, from a historical point of view, women have developed a more reflexive and inward attitude due to their social role traditionally evolving around domestic affairs and community chores in the village. But man developed more extrovertedly because his main role in the community was to be open to the surroundings, as he was responsible for hunting and keeping the family safe and secure.[61] So, it may be possible that, for woman, the act of embellishing becomes an extroverted compensation for her usual introverted disposition. But the need to appear more beautiful may flow into vanity; that is, it may constellate the shadow of the introverted feminine disposition inherent to her historical development. And there, a woman may become herself an easy prey of her own desire to catch the most attractive man out there.

In contrast to this, when we observe the animal world, we see that the males tend to be "naturally" more embellished than the females. With few exceptions, the male is physically more exuberant in size, strength and colors, and is a much greater exhibitionist during courting season. Among zoologists, this is very well understood, for the male is attracted to the female in a different manner as compared to the way the female is. The male must present himself physically more attractive to the female, for it is she who will decide upon the partner in order to propagate the offspring. In the case of human beings though, especially at an adult age, it is the woman who usually decays sooner as compared to man, physically speaking, because all hormonal changes, childbearing and breastfeeding she goes through in life. It is not

---

[61] B. Hannah, *The Inner Journey – Lectures and Essays on Jungian Psychology*, 43.

absurd then to think that, historically, woman had accounted on artificial means to enhance her attractiveness. Therefore, considering that this is a condition somewhat less conscious and possibly more compensatory, women seem to be more prone to surrender to the imprisonment imposed by cosmetic activities, at least in former times.

From a man's perspective, the substitution of the maiden by her shadow further reveals that the stage of development of his relation to woman, to the feminine and to the Anima is still quite faulty. It means that a man such as this must first be entangled with a real woman in order to realize the sensual, juicy and earthy aspects of the feminine before reaching its Anima quality. Hardly a man, if any, can approach "his" anima without "inter-coursing" with a real woman. One of the damaging consequences of the failure to undergo such an experience is what can be seen among celibate religious men (or men with an overpowering mother complex). By trying to lift up their bodies and their devotion to where they project their souls, they become neurotic and prey to perverted sexual acts, fantasies and victims of witch-like women. Quite often they develop autoerotic behavior so that all creative possibilities will not flourish. If man avoids "knowing" (also in a biblical sense) a woman, his Anima may also act accordingly to him. That is, besides revealing herself not mature enough to perform her role as a spiritual guide for him, the Anima may act mostly in a negative and destructive way. There is a Brazilian pop music writer, José Ramalho, who properly said that when he sang, *"Only that man who has penetrated the thousand maidens, the many Magdalenes, maybe knows and will know about himself."*

The triangle composed by the Mooress, the maiden and the prince can be analyzed from both point of view: the feminine or masculine psychology. In the first scenario, as mentioned, the Mooress appears as the shadow of the maiden, and in the second case, both the Mooress and the maiden appear as features of the prince's Anima.

When reading in the tales that the Mooress either kills or tries to kill the maiden with a needle or by sticking a pin into her temple (ears, forehead, head, or eyes, depending on the version), it shows clearly the harmful aspect of the shadowy contents that have not yet been integrated. Marie-Louise von Franz expands on the motif of the pin/needle in fairytales, emphasizing some important aspects.[62]

From the point of view of the language, as Marie-Louise von Franz highlights, the expression "to prick somebody" indicates that someone's personal complexes have been affected by spiteful comments of men or women aimed to cause harm, just like witches. In the ancient activity of casting spells upon someone, the main instruments or tools to perform such a deed are composed of needles, plant thorns, stones, bones or pointed spikes, which were poked into the person. Consequently, the shaman's work was to remove those objects so that the person's health could be restored. It is quite common in fairytales to see a character put to sleep, almost always through the use of a needle, often introduced behind the ear, or else the character pricks himself or herself on a pointed object (remember the tales "The Sleeping Beauty" or "The Princess and the Twelve Pairs of Golden Shoes"). Thus, the use of pins and needles has the power to cause harm to the individual or to blunt his conscious activities. In the Caribbean region, the Voodoo practitioners use the same idea, although telepathically, since the person whom they wish to affect is not pricked directly, but the doll representing the victim.

On the positive side, needles are very useful instruments, as one can see by the millenary Chinese practice of acupuncture. By inserting needles on the meridians for healing purposes, they help the body to restore the harmony that has been lost. It is also by means of hollow needles that medicaments are injected into the body for therapeutic reasons. Therefore, we must not fail to consider that upon sticking the needles into the maiden, something of the Negress may also be injected into her. Needles have also been used, since ancient times, in sewing activities, and for that matter they are related to an aspect of Eros, since they "unite" pieces of cloth (or leather) to dress up and to protect a person.

---

[62] M.-L. von Franz, *Archetypal Patterns in Fairytales*.

In the tales analyzed here, however, a needle has been used in its negative aspect to injure that region of the body where thoughts and ideas originate. This means that, by introducing the needles into the head, the plot goes beyond a simple death: the aim is the annihilation of the inspiring capacity inherent to the Anima's functioning. In other versions, the needles are driven into the eyes or ears, and this can be metaphorically understood as a mutilation of the capacity for seeing or hearing — an ability the Anima would bestow to the prince. In Oedipus, by pricking his own eyes, he annihilated himself; that is, the pins were used, metaphorically speaking, for self-castration. In this myth, we find the masculine principle succumbing since its relation to the feminine principle becomes unsuitable, therefore, a non-prolific relationship. What he really injures is his *phallus*, the masculine creative potential which was not yet fully developed or made conscious as far as it is required for a more sound relationship to the feminine.

Nevertheless, the maiden does not die, but is turned into a bird. She is no longer human but a "spiritual" being instead. This is actually a typical situation observed whenever new psychic content dawns but is not fully embraced by consciousness; it regresses back into the unconscious. It is important to note, though, that the maiden does not return to the fruit from whence she came in the beginning. This is relevant, for it demonstrates that, in spite of a certain regressive movement, this function is not too far from consciousness as compared to while she was entrapped in the fruit. The backward step in the tale seems to be related to the need for further maturation of the contents so that progression may take place next. Knowing that the princess has turned into a dove leads one to believe the Anima had become too spiritualized, and consequently, Eros appears as something ethereal and ghost-like, contrary to the kind of Eros heralded while the princess was entrapped in the fruit. The latter erotic possibility was more concrete, more sensual in a way, but now, the prospect for relatedness to the feminine goes through the air and, therefore, still in need of redemption.

The presence of these witch/negress/mooress/saracen aspects of the Anima in the Christian man reiterates the dissociative character of the catechesis inherited from the Courtly Love man. That is, the unredeemed side of this Anima forces the split in the feminine so that man perceives woman either too low (as a prostitute or snake) or too high up (as a dove or a saint). And this may be one of the greatest disappointments women hold against men. Rarely a man harmonizes with the whole set of octaves which comprises a woman's (and Anima's) gamut.

This allegorical situation occurs quite often in analytical practice. Often times, even though some contents belonging to a complex may have been integrated by consciousness, the individual eventually falls for the traps such powers have to ensnare him or her. The individual sees himself or herself again entangled in a given situation or victimized by the affects. But such a regression does not mean, necessarily, a complete disaster. Rather, it must be understood that a further upgrade in consciousness is required. More reflection, pondering on the *pathos* imposed by the complex still requires further understanding.

From this moment on in the story, we find this very situation of "regression," for now the prince has to marry the Mooress — the negative aspect of the feminine. It should be said that this is what happens to a man anytime he fails to care adequately for newly born Eros. It feels to him like a defeat or surrender to the dark side of the feminine. He is not willing to marry; he just has to! Besides, there is no human power equal to the witch's! Such a *connubium* must be undertaken for the sake of his psychic totality. But even though this situation could be characterized as a capitulation, the Ego must still stand guard and watch out for the negative mother-complex so that is does not spoil the maturation process of his Anima/Eros.

Such a passage in the fairytale is very meaningful for it gives us an indication of how much the prince has grown and matured since leaving his parents' home. He now honors the commitment he proposed before and accepts the "vile" task. He abandons his childish disposition and embraces an adult life, one which is more committed. This attitude is a symbolic representation of how fundamental it is, especially in man's psychology, that the masculine retains the capacity to endure, to resist backsliding and performs his inner duties, all while bearing the burden of the opposites inside himself. For only then may his creative potential flourish. Of course, what has just been said seems to be quite idealistic. But it is actually the only thing left to be done; there is no choice — fate has imposed this ordeal on the man. He either takes it or falls back to the powers of the great and devouring Mother.

This is a *sine qua non* condition for the individuation process. The Self, in its role of impelling us to become "whole," thrusts upon us the almost unbearable task of accommodating the polarity of the opposites within ourselves. In the tale, this situation is perfectly illustrated when the prince returns to the palace accompanied by such a horrible woman instead of the beautiful maiden. He introduces her to his parents, and even so, a wonderful wedding party is given. In other words, the royal couple, an allegory of the Self, celebrates this "spurious" union that seems to be necessary for the development of the plot, and, in the end, of the prince himself.

Well, in spite of trying to destroy the promising inspirational capacity of the maiden, the Mooress was not completely successful for, upon turning her into a dove, the beautiful girl acquired an autonomous aspect without losing completely her disposition. She hovers around the palace, until the prince overhears the truth about the usurpation and the treachery that befell him. This is a significant passage, for it illustrates a psychological condition essential to the process of transformation. It reveals that, at a certain moment, it becomes necessary that the Ego yields and embraces the negative aspect of Anima, without being reluctant or making a fuss. For that could be the only way the positive aspect of the Anima may eventually express itself more freely. This condition illustrates the "sacrifice of the intellect" in favor of a higher level being reached by the individual. As Marie-Louise von Franz states, when the individual sacrifices what is most precious to him, he has the chance to envision the true meaning of his life.[63]

Symbolically, the dove, being a bird, is frequently associated with spiritual contents, also gravid because it inspires. In Pagan

---

[63] M.-L. von Franz, *Animus and Anima in Fairy Tales*, 38.

times, the dove was also an attribute of Aphrodite/Venus, for it symbolized constancy and love, thus being essential for the completeness of psychic life. The situation in the fairytale, therefore, is quite significant from the point of view of psychic development. We can see here that, in the specific case of the man, once he is incapable of taking hold of his relationship with the feminine, it escapes; it then turns into a bird and flies away. As long as the eros-image in a man is a dove, he is but fantasizing about what a real woman is. The feminine, and more specifically, the Anima is still only a psychological concept. Contrarily, the Anima is real — she is the objective psyche who shapes and defines, for better or worse, the destiny of a man!

An analogous condition can be observed in a dream of Jung's which he mentions on several occasions in his work. Jung's understandings of his own dream bring in another dimension to what has been shown in the fairytale:

> *I was sitting on a gold Renaissance chair; in front of me was a table of rare beauty. It was made of green stone, like emerald ... Suddenly a white bird descended, a small sea gull or a dove. Gracefully, it came to rest on the table, and I signed to the children to be still so that they would not frighten away the pretty white bird. Immediately, the dove was transformed into a little girl, about eight years of age, with golden blond hair. She ran off with the children and played with them among the colonnades of the castle ...The little girl returned and tenderly placed her arms around my neck. Then she suddenly vanished; the dove was back and spoke slowly in a human voice. "Only in the first hours of the night can I transform myself into a human being, while the male dove is busy with the twelve dead." Then she flew off into the blue air, and I awoke.*[64]

---

[64] C. G. Jung, *Memories, Dreams and Reflections*, 171.

According to the information given in the introduction of the *Red Book*, Jung wrote in the *Black Book 2* that this dream made him embark on a relationship with a woman he had met three years beforehand (probably Toni Wolff).[65] It must be said that this dream occurred in a moment of Jung's life when confrontation with the unconscious was inexorable. It was the time after he broke up with Freud, when he felt a deep need to find again the revivifying sources of life.

Jung understood that the dove/girl in the dream was a symbolic representation of a condition he must relate with during his own inward journey. Symbolically, the part of his soul personified in the dove and revealed in the figure of the girl for short periods of time could become bonded to the unconscious forever if not welcomed right away. Jung, different from the prince in the tale, does not allow the prospective redemption possible through his meeting with Miss Wolff to fly off.

In the more simplified versions of the tale, the dove infiltrates the palace until she makes the cook, the gardener or some other servant understand the whole plot. Then the prince, through different maneuvers to attract the dove, manages to hold it in his hands, finds the pin and takes it out. The dove regains her human form; the Mooress is exposed, and the prince marries the maiden. But in other versions, they still go through a lot of trouble before the marriage happens.

In "The Story of The Crooked Mooress," "The Three Citrons of Love" and also in Ruth Guimarães' version ("The Little Dove and The Crooked Mooress"), the dove is caught by means of a snare. Actually, she is not caught, rather she decides to step into the snare, which was ordered by the prince to be made by the cook/gardener. The first snare is made out of a cheap material, like a thread or a ribbon, which the dove refuses. Then, the value of the trap must be continuously upgraded (silver, gold, pearls or diamond) until she finally decides that it is worthy enough for her. Again, this passage illustrates that whatever she may eventually represent, it is psychically precious, so she can only be caught by

---

[65] C. G. Jung, *The Red Book – Liber Novus*, Philemon Series, 98.

something of similar value to her own. But in the version of "The Story of the Crooked Mooress" by Romero, the snare she asks for does not meet her standards. After being offered another snare made of gold, she rejects it as well and demands one made of birdlime. This is somehow surprising because, comparing to silver, gold or diamond, birdlime conveys no value and is allegedly considered a cruel way to trap birds.

Birdlime is an old preparation utilized since ancient times to catch birds. It is a sticky material which is prepared by cooking the latex obtained from different species of plants for several hours. This substance is then spread on branches or twigs so that when the bird lands in, it is "glued" there. In many countries this practice has been now forbidden by law for being considered too cruel. We must ask ourselves why, in this version, the little dove requests this way to be captured. Traditionally, in the southern European countries, the birdlime is prepared from the latex obtained from the holly tree. This tree, more specifically the European holly (*Ilex aquifolium*) is often related to Christmas time, and in pre-Christian cultures to winter solstice. It is a plant capable of resisting winter cold and snow without losing its green tonality. It is a token for that which endures. Therefore, by instructing that she may be ensnared only by a lace made of birdlime, the dove conveys that she is herself a kind of value capable of lasting, that she can endure the most inhospitable conditions of life. Thus, if a man is properly "instrumented" to get hold of his Anima, no matter how cold or snowy his wintery inner life at times may be, he will always know that something inside himself is still fresh enough, supporting him, announcing brighter days to come.

In the "Bél Princess" version, what can be observed is that instead of sticking a pin into the maiden's head, the cunning woman pushes her into a well, and she becomes a lotus flower that no one can reach, except the prince. The image of the lotus flower blooming in water is a widespread metaphor in the East which points to the realization of a potentiality that requires profound inner work. Many images of Buddha are shown either seated or standing upon the lotus, suggesting that he is the utmost development of the plant growing up out of the darkness and produces light.[66] The lotus flower that sprouts from Vishnu's navel, for example, represents the creation of the universe starting from the "Central Sun" — the central point of the "unmoving motor." Besides, this flower, before appearing on the surface, germinates in the muddy bottom of the lake, gradually making its way up to the top. Hence, the lotus is looked upon as that which is realized out of chaos.

So in this version of the fairytale, it becomes more evident that the prince's meeting with that which is fundamental for the completeness of his psychic economy requires a sober inner work. He must mature within. Up to now, the prince has been searching in the outer world for the means to recover the maiden. From then on, she will be at his side all the time, but he will only notice her after he suffers her loss. By "suffering" it is meant that the libido makes a movement towards introversion so that the inner "motives," Ego aspirations and the demands from the Self can be clarified. That is, the individual must endure the conflict inside! He must then grow out of the "mud," which means that he must outgrow the spurious matrimonial partnership he embarked upon with the villain woman he betrothed.

This situation is quite different from the one seen at the beginning of the tales. Here, the prince has been "touched" by the numinosity of the princess. So, if at the beginning of the tale the prince was suffering from an existential void, now his pain is due to the loss of what he felt to be a fundamental part of himself. The latter "suffering" seems to be more prospective; it "makes sense," and maybe for this reason the princess insists on being present in one way or other. Expanding this perspective a little more, it can also be said that the suffering of the prince now is "less unconscious" and therefore less neurotic or paralyzing. It is a suffering with meaning!

But the masculine principle in the prince in these tales is not sufficiently conscious yet. He picks up, for example, the lotus flower and hands it over to his cunning wife, and she immediately

---

[66] C. G. Jung, *Visions: notes of the seminar given in 1930-1934,* edited by Claire Douglas, Vol 2, 1002.

"knows" that this flower is the maiden she pushed into the water. In this version, the prince continues to be a victim of the negative Anima and of his own ingenuousness (the play of the mother complex). This is emphasized by the fact that, in other versions, it was either the gardener or the cook who were responsible for dealing with the dove. And, as it could not be otherwise, it was the Saracen/Negress/Witch who surges forward in order to interfere with the encounter between the prince and the maiden. In these versions, we could say that both the gardener and the cook are nuances of the prince's shadow, which, in the final instance, shows that he is not in the "know." Therefore, he must pay for his lack of conscience and his immaturity.

It is not without reason, then, that the maiden, in the form of a dove, should present herself to the gardener/cook, and not directly to the prince himself. Symbolically, it means that the meeting of the individual with his soul, or with the most genuine aspects of his existence as a being, must go through an assimilation of the inner contents that work autonomously within him, that is, his shadow, his idiosyncrasies, as such. But as this "soul" is still in the form of a bird, this indicates that the process has not come to an end yet. Many things will happen still, as we have seen and will continue analyzing.

The figures of the gardener and the cook are positive shadows for the prince, though, since they do not act in opposition to him. Such professions are linked to Eros, since one takes care of plants and their growth, while the other works with the preparation of food. Both activities can be associated with the capacity for establishing, strengthening and nurturing relationships. But these contents, being unconscious (the shadow), are susceptible to the dark powers of the unconscious because they are still there. In other words, instead of having a positive effect on the development of the story, they are overtaken by the obscure figure of the negative Anima and end up becoming her partners in spoiling the "meeting" between the prince and the prospective figure of the maiden.

In "The Love of the Three Pomegranates" and "The Three Citrons" versions, we observe that, as soon as the Black Queen discovers that the little dove is actually the beautiful maiden, she orders it to be captured, killed and cut into pieces. This is evidence of the underdeveloped erotic capacity of the prince – considering that it is still projected in the figure of the cook who yields to the dark Anima. He manages to "catch" the dove again, but this only shows that she will fall once more under the claws of the negative aspect of the Anima. From the feathers and spoils of the little dove thrown in the garden, miraculous trees start to grow outside, bearing gorgeous fruits ready to be harvested. In "The Three Citrons," the tale is almost over before the prince learns about all the ordeals the maiden went through. At this point, he does not move away from the maiden, but soon marries her. So here the masculine principle seems to have learned that those contents can no longer be abandoned to their own fate.

As the maiden in these versions is sacrificed once more, this means that, being representative of the Anima of the prince, she also needs to go through a maturing process. That is an important psychological feature, for every time an individual becomes aware of an aspect of the Anima, a new kind of relationship with this psychic function is established. After this relation begins, there occurs a transformation in the dynamics of the conscience, which engenders a new perception in man. Therefore, a different nuance of the Anima must also be assimilated. Marie-Louise von Franz illustrates this situation when she discusses four stages related to the inner feminine experience a man goes through during his psychic development: *"The first stage relates to the figure of Eve, because the instinctive and biological urgency is very intense. The second refers to the figure of Helen of Troy, who impersonates an aesthetical, romantic level, although still linked to sexual contents. The third stage is represented by the Virgin Mary, for her figure elevates love (Eros) to the most sublime level of spiritual devotion. And the fourth stage is symbolized by Sapientia (Sophia), for it faces the kind of knowledge that transcends what is most sacred and pure."*[67] In other words, when observing the progress of man

---

[67] C. G. Jung, *Man and His Symbols,* Chap. 3, "The Process of Individuation," M.-L. von Franz, 181.

towards his totality, or towards the realization of his essence as an individual, his relation to his inner opposite, that is, with his soul (or his internal feminine figure), goes through different stages. This occurs because the inherent "requirements" of the process of development presumably have distinct levels of assimilation. They begin with a biological urgency and proceed towards a deeper awareness of the most divine image each one has within. In Jungian language, this is the Self; in religious life, God; or the center of transcendental wisdom.

Actually, what Marie-Louise von Franz proposed above is, in general terms, the development of the relationship between man and "his" Anima figure, in a rather schematic way. It does not mean, however, that these are the absolute representations, or that these are the only unfoldings of the Anima figures. In the fairytale discussed here, it can be seen that the feminine appears dichotomized, that is, the good and evil aspects are separated, quite in accordance with the manner in which the Christian world is conceived. The tale tries to bring together these aspects of the feminine inside the psychic economy of the prince, and each one goes through a process of progression/regression, according to how the tale unfolds. The Slave/Negress/Saracen occupies the place of the queen, but is eventually discovered and is sent back, at least partially, to the unconscious (partially because it depends on the ending of each version of the tales, as will be discussed further ahead). The greatest task, though, belongs to the Ego which must strive to hold together the opposition between the chthonic and heavenly representations of the feminine. For there are certain gradations of these representations which may never be integrated in a personal way, as it would be dangerous for a mortal to try to come too close to such goddesses. The Ego should not try to conquer the evil aspects of the Negress, but to unmask and eventually to debunk them. The same applies to the saintly aspects of the Virgin Mary. The Ego should not try to marry her nor try to find her representative here on Earth to make his wife. Such goddesses must be revered and propitiated for what they convey of our psychic contents, negative or positive, but one should not try to find them objectively in real life.

The maiden, on the other hand, initially hidden in the fruit, becomes a bird, dies, is reborn, becomes human again, and then assumes the place of the queen. Each one of these developments corresponds to what level of relationship the prince has with his Anima and his given consciousness at different moments within the story.

Therefore, considering that the figure of the prince is more in line with the dominants of the collective consciousness and that, in the development of the tale, he goes through a transformation process, the figures which are more connected to unconscious contents (the different aspects of the Anima) also go through a correlating process. We can observe, then, a reciprocity in the development of the contents of both consciousness and the unconscious.

This condition is exemplified in clinical practice by the dreams of a middle-aged man with great difficulties, not only with women in general, but also with the internal figure of the Anima. At the beginning of analysis, his dreams showed a huge urge to have sexual intercourse with black women, domestic servants, or other socially low-ranked women. He eventually dreamt of a "saintly," fat and quite chthonic black woman, thus showing how sacred the "despised" elements are, although always vital for unification of the personality. This man felt that he must bow devotedly before such contents. As he continued with his analytical process and engaged in more vivifying experiences with the feminine, he started to dream about renowned feminine figures, fashion models, very beautiful and "white" women. This meant that this man was experiencing within himself different aspects of the Anima, once he became more aware of his inner processes. (In this specific case, there was still an enatiodromic feature to be observed with this dreamer, as he goes from one aspect of the Anima to its very opposite.)

In the "Love of The Three Pomegranates" version, the prince still has to wait a little more before acquiring the necessary clarity to take hold of his relationship with the maiden. The pomegranates growing on the tree in the prince's garden have a magical feature, since it is said that if a sick person were to eat these fruits, his or her health would be restored and life spared. The presence of the pomegranate in this tale, therefore, is related to the aforementioned symbolism of the fruit as far as its revivifying characteristic is concerned. In this version, it is evident that the feminine, again entrapped in the fruit, is at the service of the Self, as it promotes healing.

Thus, in this tale, the last pomegranate that was plucked remained in the house of an old woman, who, unfortunately, was unable to take it to her husband in time to cure him from his illness. This passage is of vital psychological importance, for it demonstrates that the "psychic medicine" does not cure indiscriminately, just by knowing that it exists. Sometimes, analysts attend to patients referred by other patients who had had "good results" with their psychic development during analysis. The newcomer, then, expects to obtain the same "medicine" his or her friend received. This does not always happen, for each person is a receptacle for the specific remedy his or her psyche is in need of, and — mostly importantly — one should not forget that "work" must be done. It is only after a deep and sober inner scrutiny that the individual medicine can be found and administered.

Returning to the tale, it is important to emphasize that it was the prince who made the usurping Queen hand the fruit over to the old lady, thus indicating that the masculine principle has now acquired some assertive power. This is a significant detail, as it reveals that, in its relation with the figure of Anima, either negative or positive, the Ego must find a certain standpoint of its own, so it will not become obliterated or possessed by such content. As an archetypical entity, the Anima also needs the consciousness/Ego to be realized. So it is vital for the Ego to establish a "dialogue" with such figures, so that, *data venia*, it makes its point, set boundaries, and does not get lost within the archetype.

In this manner, now that a more positive move has been made on the part of the prince (through the element most associated with consciousness — the Ego), something more prospective is also constellated in the unconscious. The old lady keeps the pomegranate for decoration, but every day when she goes out to church, the maiden steps out of the fruit and does all the house-work. This reflects a new eros attitude which has been developed.

Eventually, the old lady comes to know about the maiden's ordeals. She then dresses the girl appropriately and takes her to church for Sunday's mass, so she can be seen by the prince. He recognizes her, finds out about the whole plot, and the tale progresses up to the marriage of the prince with the maiden, and the annihilation of the usurping Saracen.

The unfolding of this narrative clearly shows the prospective movement in the unconscious through the development of the figure of the maiden. In a proper environment and even without any help, she is capable of reappearing from the pomegranate. She is more humanized, as she does all the domestic work and is seen as being more "qualified" for social life. As we have already seen, if a given content has made a positive impression upon the conscience, but the Ego is not fully prepared to embrace it, such a content tends to recede once more into the unconscious. Nonetheless, its "memory" may still be present in consciousness, and its emulation from unconscious could be somewhat less difficult.

There is, however, still another important aspect in this version, associated with Christian influence. Here, the final redemption of the maiden is completed in the church, that is, under Christian principles. And the Christian solution for the conflict with the demon, as we know, is to exclude it. In some versions, there are indications that the contents represented by the Mooress have been sent back again to the unconscious, although this does not necessarily mean that it will "disappear." The Negress of several versions ends up being executed in public, in a similar way to what used to happen to the medieval witches. But she continues very much alive in the unconscious. Anyhow, as we will see ahead, there are signs that, on some level, the features of the villain Mooress have not been completely banished.

THE RENEWAL OF THE ANIMA

Among the variations of the tales we have studied, the "Bél Princess" version could be considered the most suitable for the task of interpretation. For, besides having all the elements present in the other versions, it also brings us others that greatly enrich the understanding of the psychic functions discussed here. In this version, after throwing the lotus petals in the garden, a quince tree grows, and only the prince can pick up the unique and marvelous fruit it bears. But, once more, he leaves the quince on the table (hence, without the necessary care), and his cunning wife throws it into the garden. During the night, the fruit splits open and from inside it comes a beautiful girl who the gardener takes home and cares for as if she were a gift from God.

Up to now, we have one-sidedly emphasized that it was the prince's immaturity and incapacity for growth that caused him to be betrothed to the usurping woman. In principle, this situation points to the fact that there exists a "deficiency" inherent to the prince, and he pays for it by being obliged to marry the Negress. However, considering the totality of his being, it clearly means that his life needed to be revivified in the lower levels, by the rejected contents which had been so far excluded from his conscious psychic economy.

This is reinforced by the development of the lotus, since it is a plant that needs to reach the mud below to bring forth its magnificent flower to the surface of the lake. The allegorical association might be true since positive outcomes observed in the tale only appeared after the prince goes through such an experience of the symbolical mud. We have then the reappearance of the beautiful girl with solar characteristics which means, according to Marie-Louise von Franz, that a new form of life has been constellated from the deeper layers of the unconscious. The girl incorporates aspects of the Self, not only for being perceived as an answer to the prayers made to God by the childless couple, but also because she eventually placates their pain and acts in an extraordinary manner while redeeming the prince. Marie-Louise von Franz asserts that *"whenever the symbol of the Self appears as a child, it means that it arises in the spontaneity of the human being in his processes of life, although with not much theory or spiritual capacity in the collective conscience to be integrated or even named. It is one more possibility, one more event yet not realized.*"[68] And, by being a "child," it is under a double risk of perishing since, as we have said before, every time something positive is constellated in the unconscious, there is the danger that the conscience will stiffen against such newness. Also, because it is a child, it indicates that its development must be tended; it is something to be looked after.

Thus, after a period of seven years, the girl who was blossoming in the gardener's house arouses suspicions in the evil wife of the prince. Recognizing in the girl the maiden whose place she had stolen, she begins to plan a new strategy to get rid of her.

The tale emphasizes, then, this period of a seven-year in which the subsequent event incubate. From a symbolic standpoint, the number seven marks a cyclic period. A week finishes and begins again on the seventh day. God created the world in six days and rested on the seventh. The menstrual cycle goes through multiples of seven. The Sabbatical holidays occur when seven years of work are completed, and so on. Seven is also the number of steps on the astrological stairway through which the individual ascends to Heaven. Therefore, the number seven presumes continuity after an ending. As it can be seen in the tale, a cycle in the life of the prince is over, that period of time in which he had to bear and to conform to his marriage. However, from then on, a new crisis is established.

The villainous wife orders the girl to be killed. Two servants take her to the forest, meaning here that this is a new attempt to obliterate or press down into the unconscious the recently constellated content again. But they are incapable of performing the task. They try to spare the girl's life, but something unexpected happens. The girl seizes the knife from the hands of the servant and begins a process of self-cutting. She plucks out her eyes; one becomes a parrot and the other, a mynah. She also pulls out her

---

[68] M.-L. von Franz, *Individuation in Fairytales*, 27-28.

heart, and it transforms into a magnificent tank of water; her body then turns into a splendid palace with gardens; her legs and arms evolve into the pillars of the verandah, and her head changes into the dome on the top of the palace.

These unfoldings in the tale are quite tragic and shocking. They make us feel that this epilogue does not match the initial parts of the tale. But, most of all, they show the urgency of the events to be realized and mark a certain climax in the development of the plot. The tale then is arranged in an uncommon way, for the one who is supposed to be the source of redemption for the prince actually immolates herself. So, the tale makes the girl the figure of sacrifice/sacrificer *par excellence*.

The fact that the girl sacrifices herself is interesting from the point of view of interpretation because it demonstrates again that the characters in these narratives cannot really be understood as actual human beings. They are really "gods," or rather, functions and are thus a representation of a psychic disposition whose purpose is still to be understood as factors indispensable to the process of fostering the individual's inner life. And so, what could be the psychological meaning of these acts in the fairytale?

Psychologically, the self-sacrifice is almost universally associated with the idea that he or she who offers his or her life does so because he or she knows, or feels, that his or her surrender complies with a higher and unifying order. But it should also be clear that there may be, on the part of the one who sacrifices himself or herself, some sort of consciousness anchored in the Self which knows that such a "death" is temporary. This immolation then becomes purposeful, and being so, will not just signify a perishing. Jung says that the sacrifice should be perceived as a total loss of what is being sacrificed, and hence, self-sacrifice implies that, upon losing oneself, the sacrificed one also gains, for only he who possesses himself owns himself: "*the sacrifice proves that you possess yourself, for it does not mean that you are just allowing yourself to be taken; it actually means conscious and deliberate self-render, proving that you have complete control over yourself, that is, of your ego."*[69] Therefore, the self-sacrificed one will always be resuscitated by the very cause that led him or her to sacrifice.

Obviously, even if we were interpreting this and the other tales based mostly on woman's psychology, the girl in this tale could not be taken as identical to the Ego. Instead, she represents that which is regarded as the most treasured good, as far as the tale is concerned. As mentioned before, she incorporates the image of the Self, which is both the sacrifice and the sacrificer.

Then, when we analyze the sacrificing act of the girl in the fairytale, we understand that its purpose is to allow some sort of organization of what has been disharmonic in the tale. In this act, one can see that in spite of the dismembering — through the dissociation of her body — there is actually a deep pull towards unification of the contents that are falling apart. First, we must remember that the figure of the devilish wife is vitally important for the process to unfold. She has a diabolic character, as we said before, since she separates and destroys. But while she pulls towards separation, there is this reactive force within the unconscious which engenders unification. This is really an antinomycal condition because while the polarization threatens a psychic shattering, the Mooress incites union at the same time. The girl, therefore, "integrates," as such, the ruses of her shadow. In other words, she follows the orders of the Black Queen precisely, and while she immolates herself, she becomes the redeemer of the prince.

The figure of Christ may be an important parallel to this sacrificing act of the girl, as He is the image with the greatest appeal in the Western culture, for having given His life in self-sacrifice. One of the most central ideas in the Christian catechesis is that *"Christ died for our own salvation."* Literally, Christians are saved by the wine and bread transubstantiated from the body and blood of the crucified Christ. That means that a divine figure is being immolated so that energy can be drawn from It to sustain the lives of mankind. In other words, the immolation of Christ and the substrate obtained from his materiality are aspects which

---

[69] C. G. Jung, *Psychology and Religion*, CW 11, §390.

could eventually make sprout the great message of love of the Paraclete within the Christian flock.

Christ also had His dark brother with the same diabolic separating aspects which are also seen in the usurping Negress, although here an open conflict between Christ and Satan was not observed. Christ just "resisted" Evil. Eventually, then, He "departed" as matter from humanity, uniting Himself peremptorily in Spirit with His flock.

In the book "Passion of Perpetua,"[70] Marie-Louise von Franz writes about a concrete act of self-sacrifice, which was performed so that a new image of God could be realized. In the report of Perpetua's martyrdom, it is said that due to the clumsiness of her executioner while trying to kill her, she seizes the Roman soldier's unsteady arm and guides his sword directly to her own throat. She then became the symbol for the new faith that was beginning to grow in the Mediterranean — Christianity. She endured the greatest suffering by believing that it was through the figure of Christ and His teachings that her soul and the souls of others like her would be saved. Thus, different from Christ who sacrificed Himself for mankind, we see in Perpetua the sacrifice of a human being in favor of the Divine Image.

The figure of Christ also helps us in understanding the girl's self-dismembering act, since He is a dualistic figure. He is both man and God; that is, He could be taken as a model for Ego and Self functioning, which concomitantly immolate themselves. Upon sacrificing Himself, He consolidates a new consciousness and a new proposal of reordering the psychic activities around a unitary principle. That means the death of Christ paved the way to attenuate the autonomy of the psychic contents, leading to a turnover in cultural development which was never seen before in the history of mankind. It is as if all the powers *in potentia* in the psyche, that could express themselves before, independently and in a fortuitous manner, now began to act under the auspices of a unifying supra-ordaining center.

---

[70] M.-L. von Franz, *The Passion of Perpetua: A Psychological Interpretation of Her Visions.*

In a similar way, the figure of the girl sacrificed can be discussed in different ways because she may be taken as a prototype of distinct psychic functions. If she is seen as an Anima, her sacrifice is clearly associated to the development of a new relation between consciousness and the contents of the unconscious. In this context, the sacrifice of this Anima is also the sacrifice of a part of the Self, or better said, a renewal of its image. When said above that the first stage of development of the Anima is Eve, it indicated that the aspect most emphasized by the Self in this relationship (consciousness/unconscious) for the development of man is the fruition of the instinctive biological spectrum in his psyche. Progressively, each transformation of the figure of the Anima suggests that a new demand of the Self has been constellated; and this also means that the Self renews itself in its representation. It is not immediately clear in the tale, however, which aspect of the Self is being renewed. But if we agree that man "needed" to exclude or repress the feminine element to create culture, it does not seem implausible that the Self, in these tales, emulates the reunification of these aspects which were once united. So, the image the Self possibly points to the *coniunctio*.

In the Orphic myth of Dionysus Zagreus, we can find again this archetypal disposition of the sacrifice as related to the creative processes and development of mankind. According to one version of the myth, Dionysus was killed and devoured by the Titans, a giant race of destroyers. His heart, however, was saved and offered in a potion to Semele, which allows Dionysus to be reborn. The human beings, created from the ashes of the Titans burnt by Zeus, thus carry within them an evil part inherited from the Titans and a divine part originating from the Zagreus they devoured. The fundamental aspect of the Orphic cult is the liberation of the divine essence in human beings. Therefore, it is from the sacrifice of Zagreus that human beings are created.

The act of sacrifice involving torture and quartering seems to occur in a situation where consciousness mostly suffers the process instead of reaching it voluntarily. In a way, the Ego does not understand yet what the meaning is of it. The executioner in this case is the Self who carves up and transforms, from the unconscious itself, a *homunculus*. Hence, when analyzing the quartering of the girl/Anima, it is as if we are realizing that the "soul" of the prince is still incomplete, being a prisoner, sunk in the obscurity of the polarization of the Animae figures. Therefore, such a figure must go through a process of dissolution of its constituents.[71]

The girl then splits herself into aspects which will transform consciousness and bring a new spirit to the prince — into birds, a tank and a house with verandahs. He becomes conscious through the talking of the birds, inhabits a new conscience (the palace in the forest) and glimpses a spiritual renewal represented by the heart/tank at his disposal in the forest. The princess actually transforms herself into a mandala: her body a palace, her four limbs becoming pillars and her head the dome). Jung says that *"only through the mystery of self-sacrifice can man renew himself."*[72]

The fact that the girl's body is transformed into various objects ratifies, once more, her divine character. It is not uncommon to see in different religions and myths that a supreme being or an animal of great value is eventually sacrificed, and from each part of its body comes a new way of life, nutrition or any other important object for the cultural development of that people. In a Hindu myth, it is said that Purusha, the primeval being, allowed his body to be dismembered so that creation could take place. From his eyes originated the Sun, from his head the sky, from his breath the wind, and so on. Purusha, then, is a symbol of the sacrificial act that maintains the stability of the Cosmos. When Mithra sacrifices the most sacred animal, the bull, wheat grows from its spine; from its nose, garlic; from its blood comes wine, etc. So, when the girl sacrifices herself, it is the very Self which renews itself in a new "dwelling" for the prince.

While discussing the meaning of the Eleusinian Mysteries, Walter F. Otto pointed out that without death there wouldn't have been any procreation. Accordingly, even certain archaic peoples of today symbolically enact this drama in regular festivals. It means

---

[71] C. G. Jung, *Psychology and Religion: West and East*, CW 11, §411.
[72] C. G. Jung, *Two Essays on Analytical Psychology*, CW 7, §434.

that a mythical woman has to die in order for grain to spring from her dead limbs. And being so, it is only by initiation into her death that man become potent and life renewed.[73]

It is interesting to have a look at the objects into which the girl transformed herself because they will provide a better idea of how valuable such qualities are. Her heart, for example, is transformed into a tank of water. This may only be understood if we could identify in the Hindu culture the meaning of such a structure. In Ancient India, people believed that the forests were the mothers of the rivers and, therefore, one of the ways to pay homage to such sources was by building up tanks which would be the receptacles for this gift. It was thought, for example, that the waters from the Ganges came from the heavens, from the Milk Way and, thus, such sacred water must be contained in a tank built in a temple. The edification of tanks and aqueducts was a practice which flourished for more than 5000 years in the Hindu Valley civilization, and marked a profound development for the people, especially in terms of hygiene. In reality, the tanks were important water reservoirs which, in older times, had vital importance since the water supply in India is dependent on monsoons. A great number of tanks, especially the ones carved out of stone, were built along with the old pathways in order to provide water for travelers. In this way, when the heart of the girl is transformed into a towering tank of water, this shows that the Anima not only contains, but also offers the divine substance needed to sustain life.

As we were informed, the eyes of the girl transformed into two birds who managed to bring knowledge to the prince. This motif, though, is not restricted to Hindu folklore. In Teutonic mythology, we have the figure of Wotan who brings on both shoulders the ravens Hugin (thought) and Munin (memory). These two birds flew around the universe and brought back everything they gathered to their master. But here, in Hindu culture, the pairing of the mynah (*Gracula religiosa*) with the parrot has a different coloring, especially because in other versions these birds

---

[73] W.F. Otto, "The Meaning of the Eleusinian Mysteries" in *The Mysteries – Papers from the Eranos Yearbooks*, ed. Joseph Campbell, Bollingen Series XXX Vol. 2, 20.

are a pair of lovers. This means that more than simply offering knowledge or a certain dose of logic spirit, they are also the messengers of Eros. In a Cingalese tale (today's Sri Lanka), it is said two princes, while escaping from their stepmother's cruelty, overhear a parrot and a mynah saying that whoever kills and eats them would become a king and a prime-minister. In another story from Punjab (a region in the extreme opposite locale, northwest of India), there is this story of a man who leaves a pair of birds (a parrot and a mynah) to look after his wife while he goes out. As the mynah does not allow her to go out to meet a wooing prince, she plans to kill the bird. But the parrot finds a way to escape the cage and reach the husband to tell him everything that had happened. Therefore, the fact that the girl's eyes are transformed into these two birds testifies that the prince needs to become more conscious, but conscious mainly of the redemptive aspect of the feminine in his life.

THE FATE OF THE CROOKED WOMAN

In the versions analyzed here so far, one can see a strong tendency to punish and to banish the negative aspect of the feminine. As said before, this is a typical, but not exclusive, Christian attitude, which excelled in excluding and exorcizing what was considered to be evil. Notwithstanding, it is licit, and psychologically healthy, to banish what is considered pernicious and contrary to the development of the human being, especially when its absolute devilish tinge insinuates itself. The death of this malefic woman satisfies, somehow, the sane portion of our survival instinct.

Thus, in these versions there was a severe punishment of the Negress/Saracen/Witch/Black Queen figure when both her identity and cunningness were revealed. The hindering factor must be eliminated, pitilessly, from the psychic system of an individual as suggested by Marie-Louise von Franz. Otherwise, a man would never get rid of this complex completely, and his development will always halt at this very point.

In "The Love of The Three Pomegranates," the evil Saracen asked to be coated with pitch and to be burnt in the center of the town square. No emotion is present when the prince asks her what kind of punishment she should receive; she answers in an impersonal manner, as it so happens with archetypes. Such a procedure, however, was the ordinary manner used to annihilate witches in the Middle Ages. It was necessary that the whole community be present not only to watch the banishing of evil, but also to see her humiliation. Hence, we can see in this version that, being an expression of the archetype, the evil Saracen "knows" (and here it seems that she is the only one who knows!) she will not perish. Her "mortal" remains buried in the center of the square will abide there, as a token, in spite of the naïve community belief that they got rid of her. By "killing" this Saracen, it means that the power which may hinder the *coniunctio* is no longer active, for it has been, at least temporarily overcome by a right attitude of human consciousness. It does not mean, though, that the archetype of evil would be extinguished. Of course not. Yet, the fairytale has a way to express that there exists indeed a way of dealing with the negative Anima (for men) or with the power shadow of love (for woman).

In the "Love of The Three Oranges" version, "*they decided that the old witch would be covered in grease and then burned. They took her to the center of town and burned her.*" In other variants, she is put into a barrel with cutting objects and thrown downhill. As we can see in the above-mentioned versions, there was a cruel, but also somewhat ingenuous tendency to simply get rid of that figure. The use of pitch or grease only serves to accelerate the burning process, as the purpose of such happened in the Middle Ages.

In the "Story of the Crooked Mooress," the impostor "*was tied up to the tails of two savage mules, and died after being torn apart.*" The level of violence perpetrated against the Mooress appears to reveal, in a proportional way, the amount of trouble, disgust, and repulsiveness her behavior imposed on the community. Here, the utilization of two mules implies that the annihilation of the evil personified by her required an extra-human force of similar potency. These are animals known by their power, endurance and capability to carry loads impossible for human beings alone. This was a kind of death reported in the Roman Empire, as well as during the Middle Ages, anytime a severe and exemplary punishment was intended to be displayed.

But in the "Three Ciders" version, we can see a different ending of the tale; although the basic idea remains the same, that is, the attempt to drive out the evil. But here, the burned Dark Queen had her ashes thrown over the roof of the castle. This is quite a different solution compared to the other versions, and suggests that the deathly remains of the usurper will stay on the roof of the castle.

The roof is a part of the house designed to provide shelter and protection for human beings. It is a cultural acquisition that allowed man to move away from the caves and to organize his own dwelling place. Symbolically, it means the building up of his own identity and the structuring of his Ego. The roof protects the individual from the iniquity of the skies, and keeps him safe from the forces of nature he cannot control, such as the scorching sun, the heavy rains, the freezing snow and the darkness of the nights. This protection is even more desired when it is time to fall sleep, for then he is less protected and at the mercy of the powers of nature, preying animals and other inimical forces. The roof, then, is a mediator between man and whatever can happen to him in an insidious manner; it was then a place of reverence in primeval communities.

This reverential attitude towards the roof is even more under-standable when considering that it is, in a way, a reproduction made by man of heaven's dome. Hence, the roof/ceiling is like a private sky under which each individual or family can dwell, safe and secure. It also represents his attempt to recreate his own version of the macrocosm. Furthermore, the roof stands above the individual, that is, a region he cannot control and, therefore, is vulnerable. Somehow, the individual must protect himself from anything that might fall on his head. Symbolically, then, the roof represents a protection against whatever is superior and out of reach, and as such, it is also looked upon as sacred. Thus, here we can understand why the head of the sacrificed young girl was transformed into the dome of the castle, in the Bél Princess' version.

Throwing things over the roof of houses is an ancient habit, which harks back to the nostalgic idea of the place which is depository of something wishful. In the countryside regions of Brazil, it is not uncommon to find children who toss their milk teeth up to the roof when they are pulled out. They do that in the hope that new teeth will replace the ones which were thrown there. There is also a custom of calling for rain by spraying water over the roof of the house in order to emulate "the rain falling on it."

But there is also the custom of throwing things on the roof in order to make the dwellers sleep soundly, as if it were a spell. Amongst the inhabitants of an island west of New Guinea, there is this report about a man who takes earth from the graves of the dead and scatters it on the roof of the family of his beloved one. This is to ensure that parents remain asleep while they exchange their secrets. In other cultures, this practice has different purposes. In Peru, for example, the ashes of the bones of the deceased ones are thrown on the roof so that the owners may not wake while the thief is plundering the house. [74]

The roof is also a place where that which is unable to enter through doors or windows is brought into the house. In the Holy Gospel we read: "so they made a hole in the roof above the exact place where Jesus was, and through it they lowered the bed with the paralyzed man" (Mark 2:4). In many fairytales, whatever cannot enter the house manages to do so through the roof, as an invasion. In more ancient cultures, the roof is believed to be the area where the spirits dwell. It is also from there that those spirits get into the house, no matter whether they are good or bad spirits. Hence, different rituals usually take place on the roofs of the houses in order to propitiate these spirits.

Now, once the ashes of the usurping Negress were thrown upon the roof of the palace, this indicates that there exists, at least in principle, a certain atonement for what she represents. It

---

[74] J.G. Frazer, The Golden Bough, 29.

means, then, that there is some "knowledge" that she was not, nor could be, completely annihilated. Actually, this act numbs consciousness about the virulence of the evil and, at the same time, ratifies its potential to plunder our convictions.

It must further be said that what was thrown upon the roof was indeed the ashes of the Negress, and not something else. When instead of burying our dead we cremated them, it allowed us to keep the imperishable remains of our beloved ones, that is, their ashes, in a jar inside our house and beside us forever. So this version of the fairytale ritualizes the apparent defeat of the Negress, for her remains are not just thrown away — rather, they are given a specific destination.

For the Christian community, the ashes obtained from the burnt palm leaves consecrated on the Palm Sunday of the previous year symbolize both repentance and penitence for a capital sin. They allow the believer to renew his faith and to be reborn in Christ. Originally, the penitents used to wear special clothes during penitence and sprinkled ashes over themselves at the beginning of Lent, which starts on Ash Wednesday. Nowadays, we still find people in some Christian communities who mark their foreheads with ashes in the form of a cross, as a pledge to move away from sin and to live their lives according to the Holly Scriptures.

Lent corresponds to the period of forty days before Easter, which celebrates the Resurrection of Jesus Christ. By offering penitence, food sacrifices and the like, followers re-enact the forty days of isolation and tribulation Christ went through in the desert. Hence, the ritual with ashes in Christian communities is also associated to the idea of renewal and resurrection.

Regarding life and death, especially within the Eleusinian mysteries, the earth (γῆ - gē) or matter (ὕλη - hyle), in its simplest form — as cinis, ash of the dead — is immortal, is God. This ancient concept is again reflected by a man and woman from the Mediterranean region who, in their epitaphs, tried to convince themselves that they were ashes (*cinis*) and, consequently, were not dead. They would survive not only through but in the image of multi-breasted Ephesian goddess, Artemis:

Cinis sum, cinis terra est, terra dea est,
Ergo ego mortua non sum.[75]
(I am ash, ash is earth, earth is goddess,
Therefore I am not dead.)

Expanding on this idea a little more is the concept of the mythological bird called phoenix, which is burned but rises again from its own ashes. This means that not even fire can destroy what is meant to be regenerated. Thus, the ashes of the usurping Negress work as a reminder to the possibility of her revivification and of the danger that she may tumble down on people's heads at any time. Psychologically speaking, this shows that the psychic contents, especially those already constellated, will never be retained in the unconscious forever. This reaffirms their autonomy and demonstrates that at any time, be it for inner or outer reasons, they can make themselves known. But only when "they wish." It is in "The Three Citrons of Love" version, though, that we are openly told that the contents represented by Black Maria should not or cannot be forgotten, "maybe because she does not represent only the evil principle, but also the earthy aspect of life." It is the beautiful maiden herself who utters the manner in which her opponent must be handled: "*I want a drum to be made out of your skin, so I can play it when I go out in the street, and a ladder made from your bones for me to descend to the garden.*"

We can see a very different tendency in this version, for the feminine figure recently integrated into the conscience brings with her all the contents of her shadow, now a little bit attenuated. By the actions she suggests, she can keep the most immediate outer expression of her shadow, the skin, and also its imperishable essence, her bones. In this version, it seems that pricking pins into the maiden's temple had the effect of introducing some substance of the negress Maria into the damsel — she wouldn't be hanging naively on trees anymore, as a fruit.

---

[75] J. Campbell (ed.) *The Mysteries – Papers from the Eranos Yearbooks,* Bollingen Series XXX, vol. 2, 113.

But what could be the symbolic meaning of the princess saying she wishes to make a drum and a ladder out of Maria's skin and bones, respectively?

In the first place, it is necessary to identify some of the main functions of drums in different cultures. In a movie about the life of Joan D'Arc, *The Messenger* (1999) by Luc Besson, there is a line where she says: "*I am the drum through which God sends His message.*" Hence, as in other cultures, the drum serves to share some kind of communication. The sounds of the drums in various tribes of Indians around the world basically point to some kind of announcement: a celebration, a warning or even a war. They are also an instrument to mark rhythm, to produce music and, therefore, act as an ordering principle. It is quite well known that drums are used by Shamans to avert evil spirits. But they also used drums as vehicles to reach the necessary ecstatic state which allowed them to venture into their shamanic journeys.

The process of building a Shaman's drum involves several rituals, depending upon the tradition they belong to. However, when they have to use the leather skin of some kind of animal, that material must first be "spiritualized," so to speak. Then, when the Shaman plays the "revived" drum, he shares the theriomorphic nature of his ancestors, or emulates their characteristics.[76]

The utilization of human skin in the manufacturing of drums is not so common, although it does have a specific function in some cultures. Among the Huancar Indians of Peru, it used to be a normal practice to make drums out of the skin of their enemies, called *runatinyas*, as a means of taking hold of their power and spreading fear amongst them.

The fact that the princess asks for a drum to be made out of the Negress' skin to be played when she goes out into the street also has this declaring aspect to it, which is actually common to all drums in general. For a man, this would indicate that he now has a more differentiated kind of Anima who is now differentiated from the dark sides of the unconscious, but still able to communicate with such uncanny power. It could also be understood as a way of sharing the dark aspects that should not

[76] M. Eliade, *Shamanism: Archaic Techniques of Ecstasy*, 175.

just be repressed in the princess, in her new family and in the community, as well. In this way, the presence of the princess will always be announced alongside an aspect of the Black Woman. Symbolically, this is an important progressive development in the group of fairytales analyzed here, as we have said above.

But, it is not only in the social presentation of the princess that the figure of the Dark Woman will be emulated. The tale also says that a ladder must be made out of her bones to be used when the princess "descends" to the garden. Generically speaking, the coming together of drums and bones points to the respect due to the ones who were brave enough to go through the archetypal experience and make it. That is, we here observe a certain laureation of the transformation process which occurred in the story.

Bones are considered to be the imperishable substance of the individual after his death. According to Eliade, among the different Shamanic practices around the world, it is common to see the presence of animal or human bones attached to the Shaman's clothes. This is a condition which reaffirms the special status of the special being, since he who wears it is the one who once died, but is alive again. During his developing process and initiation, the Shaman undergoes a symbolic death and then is born again with special powers. Therefore, it is believed that the soul of the deceased still inhabits his bones, and it is possible to catch a glimpse of the resurrection of the individual through his bones.[77]

In biblical imagery, the idea that individuals can revive through their bones can be found too:

"The hand of the Lord was upon me, and carried me out in the spirit of the Lord, and set me down in the midst of the valley which was full of bones. And caused me to pass by them round about: and, behold, there were very many in the open valley; and, lo, they were very dry. And he said unto me, Son of man, can these bones live? And I answered, O Lord God, thou knowest. Again he said unto me, Prophesy upon these bones, and say unto them, O ye dry bones, hear the word of the Lord. Thus saith the Lord God

---

[77] *Ibid*, 159.

unto these bones; Behold, I will cause breath to enter into you, and ye shall live: And I will lay sinews upon you, and will bring up flesh upon you, and cover you with skin, and put breath in you, and ye shall live; and ye shall know that I am the Lord. So I prophesied as I was commanded: and as I prophesied, there was a noise, and behold a shaking, and the bones came together, bone to his bone. And when I beheld, lo, the sinews and the flesh came up upon them, and the skin covered them above: but there was no breath in them." (Eze: 37:1-8)

Thus, the presence of Black Maria's bones is an uncontestable allusion to the fact that her essence did not perish. However, there is a particular aspect here, for a ladder was built from her bones in order to allow the princess to get into the garden. It is then important to analyze these details further, as they reinforce the idea that what pervades the Dark Woman is not perishable.

Ladders, in general, establish a certain *transitus*, allowing what is above to reach what is below, and vice-versa. In the book "The Passion of Perpetua," Marie-Louise von Franz analyzes the ladder which appears in Perpetua's dream and amplifies this motif through the ladder which appears in Jacob's dream (Gen 28:12), and in the visions of Zozimos. They served as a vehicle for spiritualization, a transformation of matter into a spiritualized content. But, differently from these two ladders, the tonic of the princess is the descent instead.

The ladder here conducts the princess to the garden; therefore, it leads down to earth, and consequently, to materialization. In a certain way, even though the Negress is dead, her bones prompted the princess to a place that is closely linked to the process of creation and generation of life, the garden. Psychologically, this means that it is through this new path, paved with the imperishable substance of the gloomy side of the feminine, that a new flourishing potential may be expressed. It can be seen then in this version, that, in a more explicit but not laudatory manner, the two aspects of the feminine are present in the psychic economy of the collective conscience of that environment.

CHAPTER 5

FINAL CONSIDERATIONS

The analysis of a given theme while examining various versions is not always a satisfactory task, considering that such a large amount of the material utilized ends up not being thoroughly investigated. On the other hand, by gathering variations of the same topic, it is possible to observe how a given aspect was primarily problematized and how it was dealt over different eras or by various cultures. Of no less importance is the opportunity to glimpse the possible solutamenitiions or developments proposed by the different versions, considering the respective cultures and historical influences. This is important since it helps us to understand the processes related to creation and refinement of consciousness.

As we have seen, the theme of the feminine entrapped within a fruit, or the like, is quite prevalent in tales around the world. Such tales depict the imperative need for restoration of this feminine and the troubles associated with this adventure. Both in man and in woman, the feminine is a psychic energy which is more prone to recede, for the feminine "matter" is much more compliant. As it can be seen in several fairytales and in many clinical practices, the feminine does not usually take a sword nor go out slaying dragons so that her function can settle down in the human psyche. Instead, her *modus operandi* is to withdraw her passion, waiting for the cause of the disturbance to dissipate so that the given aspect of the feminine energy can be redeemed. In other words, the feminine prevails and triumphs through spiritual toil, from *pathein*, which is the experience, the suffering, or the perception of the divine, that is, from the perception of the divine efficacy (αισθησεις των θεων).[78]

But it would be too naïve a view of the feminine to consider it mostly under its pliable disposition. This principle is also vengeful, sinister and deadly. It can hinder life processes by poisoning relationships anytime its prerogatives are usurped. The great trouble a man may face, particularly the Christian one, while coming to terms with his feminine soul is to recognize that his Anima has, and must be considered, along with its juicy, dove-like, pretty damsel aspect, a dark and witchy disposition. Yes, it may be right that the feminine is less prone to get hold of a sword, but it may prick, poison, lure, demonize, congeal and swallow up life whenever its due place, function and prerogatives are not honored or in some way are offended.

But, once more, it is necessary to emphasize that the analysis involving the feminine and the masculine here (like in any other psychological Jungian interpretation) does not equalize these functions nor even circumscribe them to a woman or to a man. Actually, they must be understood as psychic energies which pervade human beings, and as such, the analysis of such stories becomes a fundamental tool to better understand part of that which still has not flourished in the psyche of each individual.

It wouldn't be proper to finish these considerations without, once more, emphasizing the always active, dynamic and often conservative character of the archetype whenever a given psychic condition is constellated. This image of the feminine entrapped within the fruit and the implications adduced from these fairytales seem to be greatly alive and in need of understanding, especially in our days. For it is not only in man that the feminine is suffering, but progressively more among women.

---

[78] J. Campbell (ed.), *The Mysteries: Papers from the Eranos Yearbooks,* Bollingen Series XXX, vol. 2, 95.

APPENDIX

Synopsis 1: The Bél Princess[79]

In a distant country, there was a king with his seven sons. Six of them were married, but the seventh and youngest did not wish to get married and also did not like his sisters-in-law. He would not even accept the food they offered him. Angrily, they said he should marry the Bél Princess.

The young prince became interested in the Bél Princess, and started to search for her. He took one of his father's best horses, armed himself and set off, leaving his worried family behind. After travelling for six months, he came upon a fakir asleep in a cabin. Thinking this man could possibly help him, the prince decided to wait until he woke up. Meantime, he began to do the domestic chores while watching over the sleeping fakir, who usually spent six months of the year sleeping and the other six months awake.

When a month passed, the fakir awoke, and feeling pleased with what he saw, asked the prince what he could do to help him, as nobody ever managed to arrive at the cabin. Then the fakir confirmed the existence of a Bél Princess, but he said she lived in Fairyland, where no man can go. Nevertheless, he promised to help the prince.

The fakir made the prince wait for another month, taking care of the cabin and treating him as he would his own father, the king. When the month was over, the fakir gave the prince his walking stick and said:

---

[79] M. Stokes, *Indian Fairy Tales*.

"And now you go to Fairyland, which is one week's journey from this jungle. When you arrive, you will see a large number of demons and fairies who live there."

Then the fakir picked up some earth from the ground and put it into the prince's hands, telling him to blow on it, in order to become invisible, as soon as he saw those beings. Then he was to ride until he came to a wide plain, where he would see a tall bel tree bearing one very large fruit amongst its branches. Inside this fruit was the Bél Princess. "You must throw the stick towards the tree, and when the fruit falls, you should hide it in your shawl, without dropping it. Ride back here immediately, for as soon as the fruit falls, you will lose your invisibility, and the demons and fairies will try to reach you. But take care not to look back when they call you. Continue riding straight back here, for if you look back, you and your horse will be turned into stone, and they will take the fruit back to the tree," said the fakir.

The prince did as he was told, but when he was escaping with the bel in his shawl, he heard the demons and the fairies calling him, and looked backwards. He and his horse were immediately turned into stone, and the bel went back to the tree and hung there again.

For a week the fakir waited for the king's son, but as he failed to appear, he concluded that the prince had been turned into a stone. So he set out to Fairyland, where no one could touch him, and when he arrived at the plain, he found the prince on his horse, both turned to stone.

The fakir was sad, and prayed to God that the king's son could come to life again. He made a cut on the inner side of his little finger, from the tip to the palm of his hand, and spread his blood over the prince's forehead. He also rubbed some blood on the horse, praying all the time during this procedure for God to revive them both. The prince and his horse were then able to come to life again!

The fakir reprimanded the prince and told him he would have remained there forever had he not come to his help. They went back to the forest and stayed there for a week, after which the fakir gave the same advice to the prince, and handed him the stick and some earth.

This time, the prince did not look back, and riding fast, was able to bring the bel to the fakir's cabin. Upon arriving, the fakir immediately turned the prince into a mosquito, so he could be hidden from the demons and the fairies, who had already reached the cabin, searching for the prince. They said:

"There is a thief in your cabin." And the fakir asked: "A thief! Where is the thief? Look for him all around and take him if you can find him." They searched in vain.

The prince, after becoming human again, was ready to take the Bél Princess to his homeland. But the fakir gave him still another warning:

"Do not open the fruit while you are on the way; wait until you are in your father's house. Only in the presence of your father and mother you may open the fruit. And from inside will appear the Bél Princess."

After riding for six months, the prince arrived at his father's land, and finally reached the gardens. Then he said to himself: "Now that I am in my father's land and in the palace gardens, I'll sit down and rest a while in the cool shade, and when I am rested, I'll enter the palace." He washed his face and hands, and drank some water from the pool. Then he thought: "Now that I am in my father's lands and in his gardens, there is certainly no need to wait to enter the palace to open the bel. What danger could there be in opening it here and now?"

He opened then the bel, in spite of the fakir's warning, and out came a maiden of rare beauty. She was more beautiful than any other princess he had ever seen, so beautiful that he lost his senses when he looked at her. The princess fanned the prince and sprayed water on his face. He eventually recovered, and said to her: "Princess, I would like to sleep a little longer, for I have traveled for six months and feel very tired. After I have slept, we shall go together to my father's palace." Then he went to sleep, while the princess waited beside him.

Soon, a woman came along to fetch water from the pool. But seeing that the king's son was there with a beautiful maiden, wearing lovely clothes and jewels, greediness rose within her, and she began at once to plan a way to kill the princess and take her place.

The evil woman approached the princess, and cunningly managed to get her to exchange clothes with her, and even had the maiden lend the jewels to her. Then she invited the maiden to walk over to the gardens to the pool, so they could see how they looked after exchanging their clothes. But she pushed the princess into the pool, and then went back to where the prince was sleeping. She took the place beside him where the beautiful maiden had been.

When the prince awoke and saw beside him that horrid figure, wearing the same clothes and jewels of the Bél Princess, he wanted to know what had happened: "But what happened to you? How did you become so ugly?" And the evil woman answered: "Up to now, I have lived inside the bel. It is the bad air of this country that made me become like this and injured one of my eyes."

The prince was quite unhappy and ashamed, thinking sadly about having to present such a figure in his father's palace. His parents were very disappointed to meet such an awful creature, but even so, they made all the preparations for the wedding. The prince also said he did not know how it had come about, and reported to his parents all that had happened since he had left home: from the meeting with the fakir until the opening of the bel in the gardens, and the apparition of the most beautiful maiden he had ever seen. The wedding was carried out in all splendor, and the prince still believed he was marrying the Bél Princess.

In the meantime, the beautiful maiden, who had not perished in the pool, had turned into a pink lotus flower of rare beauty. But whoever tried to pick it could never accomplish this, for it always floated away. The king and his six older sons also heard of this flower that everyone tried to catch but never succeeded. So they went to try to get the flower, but it continuously moved away. Finally, the young prince, who had also heard about the event, decided to go himself and try to get hold of it. "I shall try to get this flower that nobody can touch," thought the prince. When he reached the pool, he bent over and stretched his hand out, and the flower came floating towards it. He proudly offered the flower to his wife.

She did not say anything, but knew immediately that it was the beautiful maiden she had pushed into the pool. The prince put the flower on his pillow, feeling very happy, but as soon as he went out, his wife grabbed the flower, crushing it to pieces and threw them into the garden. In a few days, a lovely bel tree began to grow in the garden, and soon a large fruit appeared on it, which all those in the village and in the palace tried to pick. However, the bel always moved out of reach every time anyone came near it. Even the king and his six sons were unable to get the fruit. And again when the young prince went to try, the quince simply fell into his hands! His evil wife was aware at once that the fruit was actually the Bél Princess.

The prince took the bel into the palace and showed it to his wife. But as soon as he was gone, she took the fruit and threw it into the garden. During the night, the quince opened and out came a beautiful little girl. In the morning, the gardener found her and was delighted, as he had no children. He thought that finally God had sent a small child to him and his wife.

The girl was raised by the gardener and his wife, and her beauty was spoken of all around the village, and then in the palace. But the cunning wife of the prince knowing she was the Bél Princess, soon devised another plan to be rid of the lovely maiden. When the child was seven years old, she drove away from the gardens a cow that had entered to graze on the well-tended flowers there. But this cow belonged to the evil wife of the prince and was part of the plan engendered to get the girl into trouble. Upon hearing about the "ill-treated" cow, she pretended to be very disgusted and to fall sick due to the event, making the prince decree the death of the gardener's daughter.

The prince ordered the girl to be taken to the forest and killed. His servants took her to the forest, but did not have the courage to kill her, being so beautiful. So she said: "Were you not ordered to kill me? Then do so." But seeing they could not do it, she took the knife from their hands and cut out both eyes. One became a parrot and the other, a mynah. She also extracted her heart, which became a magnificent tank for water. Her body turned into a splendid palace, with marvelous gardens, more beautiful than the king's. Her legs and arms became pillars supporting the roof of the verandah, while her head was the dome above the palace.

The servants, scared by such transformations, ran away and never told anyone about what they saw. However, nobody lived in the marvelous new palace. It remained there, in the middle of the forest, with its superb tank of water, and the lovely gardens with the parrot and the mynah. One day, during a hunt, the prince came upon the palace, and was surprised, for he had never seen it before then. "I wonder who lives here," he thought. He went in and visited the palace, and marveled at everything so well cared for, all the rooms very tidy and luxuriously furnished, all in a very well-arranged manner. As night had come, he decided to sleep right there, on the verandah.

While he was lying there, the parrot and the mynah came from the garden and landed quite near him, and then started to talk, for they wished the prince to hear what they were saying. The parrot then said to the mynah that "the prince's father was the king of the neighboring land, having seven sons and that six of them were married to six princesses, but the younger prince did not wish to marry and besides that, he did not even like his sisters-in-law." It stopped talking, and the prince was surprised at all the bird knew about him. But he was tired and fell asleep.

When he awoke, he went back home, but felt strange. He said he was not feeling well and needed fresh air, so he returned to palace in the forest. Once again, the parrot and the mynah came near him to talk. The parrot told the mynah about how the prince came to know of the Bél Princess, about his journeys in search of her, and how he found the quince and was turned into stone. At this point it stopped speaking.

The next evening, returning to this palace, the prince heard a little more of his story. But each time he heard about it, he became more discouraged, silent and gloomy. His wife then suspected that the Bél Princess was alive. She asked the prince why he always went out at night, and he answered that, because he was not feeling well, he was staying at another residence of his parents. He also said that, from that moment on, he would not sleep at the palace until he felt well again.

That evening, then, he heard from the birds the story up to the moment when he fell asleep in the palace gardens having the princess at his side. On the fifth evening, lying on the verandah once more, he heard about the evil woman who changed clothes with the princess and pushed her into the pool and how she became a lotus flower that his wife crushed to pieces. He also knew that these pieces became the quince thrown into the gardens, and that the child who came from inside the fruit was adopted by the gardener. Also, he heard that he was persuaded to have the girl killed when she was seven years old, and how the parrot and the mynah had once been the eyes of the girl. He was also informed that the tank had been her heart, and all the rest. The mynah then asked the parrot where the quince princess could be found.

The parrot answered that only the king's youngest son could find her, but he was very foolish, for he believed his evil and cunning wife was the Bél Princess. "And where is the princess?" asked the mynah. "She is here," said the parrot. "If the prince should come one day and go to all the rooms in this palace until he came to the central room, he would see the trap door right in the middle of this room. If he raised the trap door, he would see steps leading to a subterranean palace, and there he would find the princess." And the parrot emphasizes the fact that only the prince can do this: "It is by the order of God that no one but the younger son of the king may raise the trap door and find the Bél Princess!"

Next morning, instead of going home, the prince followed all the steps he had heard from the parrot. When he arrived at the subterranean palace, he saw it was even more beautiful than the one on the surface. There were many servants and a superb meal waiting to be served. In another room, he found a golden bed, covered with pearls and diamonds, and the Bél Princess was lying there, doing nothing more than praying in the sacred book day and night.

After revealing how he had been able to find her, the prince said he would go back to his father's palace to prepare everything, and then return to take her with him. He then shared the whole story with his parents, brothers and sisters-in-law, and all preparations were made to bring the Bél Princess to the palace. But before this, that evil woman should be killed, said the king.

So this was done. The king's servants took the deceiving evil woman to the forest, killed her and threw the body away. The Bél Princess returned to the palace, and a grand ceremony celebrated the wedding of the prince and the princess.

Synopsis 2: The Love of The Three Pomegranates[80]

The king's son, while slicing a piece a ricotta at dinner, cut his finger and a drop of blood fell upon the cheese. He said: "Mama, I would like a wife white like milk and red like blood." In spite of having learned that what is as white as milk cannot be at the same time as red as blood, the prince went out looking for such a woman.

Eventually, he came upon a little old man who, hearing about his search, told him again how impossible it was. However, he gave the prince three pomegranates, and warned him to open them only when he was near a fountain.

The young man continued his journey, and opened one of the pomegranates. From inside came a very pretty girl, as white as milk and as red as blood, who begged: "Dear young man, give me water, otherwise I'm Mother's dead daughter!" The prince hastily scooped up some water in his hands to give to her, but he was not fast enough. The lovely girl was dead. He opened another pomegranate, but being too slow again, the second girl died too.

Opening the third pomegranate, out came a girl more beautiful than the first two. This time, the prince threw water in her face, and she remained alive. As she was naked, he covered her with his cloak and said: "Climb up this tree and wait, while I go for clothes and a carriage to take you to my palace."

The lovely girl stayed high up in the tree near the fountain. But along came a horrible Saracen woman to fetch water. And when she dipped the clay jug into the pool, she saw the beautiful face of the lady in the tree reflected on the surface, and sighed: "Why must I, who am so beautiful, trudge home with water by the potful?" Then she broke the jug right there and went home.

When she arrived, her mistress was very angry, and told her to go back for water, and not dare to repeat the same procedure. Arriving at the fountain again, the Saracen saw the beautiful face

---

[80] I. Calvino, *Fiabe Italiane - raccolte e trascritte da Italo Calvino*, Vol. II, 449.

reflected in the water once more, and as before, thought it was herself. Feeling so beautiful still, she refused to carry out such a task, and broke the jug a second time. Her mistress threatened her again, and she had to return to the fountain with a new jug. Everything happened as before, but when the jug was broken a third time, the maiden up in the tree could not refrain from laughing.

Looking up, the ugly Saracen then saw the beautiful lady, and asked her to come down so she could dress her so that she should be more beautiful. While the Saracen was doing this, she stuck a pin into the maiden's ear. She died, and a drop of blood fell on the ground. From this drop, a wood pigeon appeared and flew away.

When the prince returned to the fountain, seeing the ugly Saracen, he couldn't believe his eyes, for he had left a beautiful lady who was white as milk and red as blood. Even so, he put the Saracen into the carriage and took her home. Then they got married.

But the little wood pigeon was always hovering around the kitchen window, trying to get news of the prince through the cook. So she asked him to make her a soup, and for this she would give him feathers of gold. After taking the soup, the wood pigeon shook its feathers, and the cook collected the fallen feathers. This happened again the next day, and the cook told the prince what was happening.

The prince asked the cook to catch the pigeon for him when it appeared again. But the artful Saracen overheard them and soon understood what was going on. So, the next morning, she pushed the cook away and caught the wood pigeon when it landed on the window-sill. Then she pricked it with a pin and killed it.

The little pigeon died, but a drop of its blood fell into the garden, and at once a pomegranate tree sprung up from it. This tree, however, had magical powers, for everyone who was sick and ate one of the fruit was cured from his disease. And there was a long line of people coming for the fruit until there was only one pomegranate left. It was the biggest of all, and the ugly Saracen said she wanted to keep it for herself. But an old woman asked her for that fruit, as her husband was ill and about to die. The Saracen did not wish to part with the pomegranate, but the prince objected to it.

So the old woman took the fruit, but it was too late. Her husband was dead. She then decided to keep the fruit for decorating her house. Every morning when the woman went to church, a girl came out of the pomegranate, lit the fire, swept the house, did the cooking and laid the table. Then she entered the pomegranate again. Coming back from church, the woman was very impressed with what she saw. She talked to the priest and told him what was going on at her house. He gave her instructions on what to do.

The next morning, the old woman said she was going to church, but remained outside the house. The maiden appeared and did all the housework. The old woman entered the house and caught the lady before she could get back into the pomegranate.

The maiden then told the old woman her whole story. The woman dressed her in peasant garb like her own, since the maiden was still naked, and on Sunday she took the lady to church. The king's son was also there and saw her. "My Heavens!" he exclaimed, "I do believe that is the maiden I met at the fountain!" He then waited for them on the way home. The old woman told him that the lady had emerged from the pomegranate he had given her.

The prince turned to the maiden and asked how she had gotten into the pomegranate, and she told him all that had happened to her. Then they returned to the palace, and the prince had the maiden tell her story once more, before the Saracen. For her punishment, the Saracen asked to be coated with pitch and burnt in the center of the town square. And the king's son married his beautiful maiden.

Synopsis 3: The Love of the Three Oranges[81]

A king and a queen had a son who did not seem to be very clever. The queen prayed to God for a solution to this, and the Lord told her to find something that could make the prince laugh. The queen had a jar of oil that she started to offer to anybody, in the hope that someone would appear and make the prince laugh. When, however, the jar of oil was already emptied, an old witch came along and asked for some. She entered the flask and became dirty with the remains of the oil. The prince laughed heartily. The witch then sentenced him: "You shall not be happy until you find the love of the three oranges!"

The prince then began to search for this love. He rode for a long time, and arrived at a gate. He clapped, and an old man came to open it. His eyelids reached to his toes. He asked the prince to use some forks to keep his eyes open. He gave the prince a couple of twigs, and said he would meet some uncommonly big witches, sweeping their ovens with their hands. In order to avoid being caught by them, the prince was to give them these twigs. Riding on, the prince met the witches, and they let him pass after he dropped the twigs for them.

Continuing his journey, the prince came to a larger gate. The same events were repeated. But this time another old man gave him some ropes, for the prince was to come upon some witches who were drawing water with their tresses; and he should give them these ropes so he could pass. All happened accordingly, and the prince went on until he arrived at an even larger gate than the second one. Here, a third old man, with eyelids much longer than the two previous ones, gave the prince one bag with bread and another with tallow. He told the prince he would meet enormous dogs, which he was to feed with the bread so they would let him pass. Then he would come to a gate with many locks that were very rusty. He would see a tower, and inside it, the love of the three oranges. He was to use the tallow on the locks and climb the tower

---

[81] T.F. Crane, "The Love of the Three Oranges" in *Italian Popular Tales*.

to reach the oranges that were hanging from a nail. He would also meet an old woman whose son was an ogre that ate all the Christians who had come there. So the prince had to be very careful.

After passing the dogs, the prince entered the tower and met the woman, who told him about her ogre son and what he would do to him. While they were talking, the ogre arrived and perceived something different in the house:

"Hey, hey, I smell a Christian!

I smell a Christian!"

His mother tried to divert his attention, and threw him a piece of meat. While he was busy with it, his mother gave the prince the three oranges and told him to escape immediately, for her son would eat him too. But after giving him the oranges, she was sorry and shouted: "Steps, throw him on the ground! Locks, crush him to pieces!" But the locks said they wouldn't, for he had given them tallow. She instigated the dogs to devour him, but they also refused, as he had fed them.

The prince then mounted his horse and rode away, with the old woman crying before him for the witches to kill him. They also refused to do this, for he had given them the ropes and the twigs. The prince rode for quite a time, and feeling thirsty, decided to open one of the oranges. From inside came a lovely girl, who said: "My love, give me something to drink!" But the prince said he had nothing for her, and the girl murmured: "My love, I shall die!" And she died immediately.

The same thing happened with the second orange. But when the prince opened the third, and a girl more beautiful than ever appeared, he gave her some water from a pool. Then he put her on the horse's back, and along with her, made his way home. When they were nearing the palace, he left the lovely maiden under two trees. One had leaves of gold and silver fruit, and the other had silver leaves and golden fruit. The prince wanted to announce his arrival at the palace and tell his mother he had found the beautiful maiden.

But while he was gone, along came an old witch offering to comb the lady's hair. She drove a pin into her forehead from one side to the other, and the lady was turned into a dove.

The queen, upon hearing from the prince that he had found the most beautiful maiden, had a splendid feast prepared for her, with many guests. But when the carriage, with a little dove on top, arrived at the entrance and everyone saw the horrible witch inside it, nobody could believe their eyes. The king and the queen tried to ease the situation by telling the prince that the lady would eventually recover her beauty. Meanwhile, the little dove flew to the kitchen balcony and started to sing:

"Let the cook fall asleep,
Let the roast be burned,
Let the old witch be unable to eat of it!"

As the food was taking so long to be served, they went to the kitchen and saw that the cook could not wake up. He himself did not understand what was happening to him. He put another roast in the oven, but the dove reappeared and sung the same song again.

Once more the guests waited until they got tired, and the prince went to the kitchen and said: "My good cook, what has come over you?" And the cook told him of the little dove and its song.

The prince went to the balcony, saw the dove and took it in his hands. Stroking its head, he found the pin stuck into its forehead and another in the top of its head. He pulled them out, and the dove changed into the lovely maiden he had left under the trees. He returned to the dining-room, showing everyone his true bride. When she told her story, the guests asked to be allowed to give their opinion as to how the witch should be punished. It was decided that she would be covered in grease and then burned. So she was taken to the center of town and burned, and the wedding was celebrated as it should have been in the first place.

Synopsis 4: The Three Citrons[82]

A king was in a terrible state because his son did not wish to marry. One day, when they were at the table, the prince cut his finger and two drops of blood fell onto the cheese. The mixing of the two colors made the prince desire to marry a woman who was white and red, just like the cheese dyed with the blood. So he set off to India, and arrived at the Isle of the Ogresses. An ugly old woman, learning of his quest, urged him to hurry, for her three daughters may find him and can put an end to his life.

The prince escaped and came to another country where he met an uglier woman than the first. She also told him of her ogre daughters. He fled again and came upon an old woman who was sitting on a wheel, with a basket full of cakes and candies. She was feeding jackasses that jumped around and kicked at the geese. This woman gave him three citrons and told him that now he would be allowed to go back home. But she said he should only open the citrons when he was near his own lands and close to a fountain.

The prince decided to open one of the citrons anyway. But when he did, he was not quick enough to give water to the beautiful lady, white as cheese and red as a strawberry, who came out of the first citron he opened. She just disappeared. The same thing happened with the second fruit. Opening the third citron, the prince managed to give water to the most beautiful lady he had ever seen. She was white as junket, with red stripes. However, he could only take her to the palace after she was properly dressed up. So he left her in an oak tree, while he went for suitable clothes and servants for the procession.

A black slave came to the fountain for water and saw the reflection of a beautiful face on the surface. Thinking it was hers, she did not wish to do that task any longer and broke the pitcher. Her mistress reprimanded her, and she had to go back. The third time she returned, the lovely lady in the tree couldn't help but laugh out loud at the fate of the Negress. After they talked and the

---

[82] G. Basile, *Project Gutenberg's Stories from Pentamerone*. Last access Dec. 2009.

lady told her story, the slave induces her to try and look better for the prince, who is coming to take her to the palace. The Negress offers to create a special hairdo for her, so she will become wiser (here it doesn't say she will become more beautiful, as in other versions). The slave sticks a pin into her head, and the maiden is turned into a dove.

The prince arrives and has to take this black slave instead of the beautiful lady. The wedding was celebrated in spite of the disappointment all around. In the kitchen, while the cook was preparing the feast, a dove appeared and asked him how the king and the slave were. The third time this happened, the cook finally went to tell the royal couple about the dove. The black slave queen ordered the dove to be captured and cooked for the feast.

The cook caught the dove, and after scalding it, he threw the hot water into the garden. Three days later, a marvelous citron tree grew where the water had fallen. After a few days more, three citron fruits appeared on the tree, just like the ones the old woman had given to the prince. So he asked the cook about these fruits, and hearing what had happened to the dove, he picked the citrons from the tree and took them to his rooms with a basin of water. The prince then started cutting the fruits, but was only fast enough to offer water to the maiden who emerged from the third citron. And thus he came to know about all the events that had occurred.

So the prince asked the guests in the palace what the punishment should be for anyone who would do any harm to the beautiful maiden he was now presenting to the court. The same question was asked of the black woman, and she answered: "Such a person should be burned and her ashes strewn on top of the castle." This was done, and the prince married the princess.

Synopsis 5: The Three Citrons of Love[83]

There was once a prince who went out hunting. Feeling very thirsty, he found three citrons and opened the first, from which appeared a lovely girl, saying: "Give me water, or I shall die."

The prince did not have any water to give her, so she died. Continuing on his way, and feeling thirsty, he opened a second fruit. Out came an even lovelier girl, who said: "Give me water, or I shall die." He still did not have any water, and this girl died too. The prince felt very sad, and went on, promising to open the third citron as soon as he could find a fountain.

Upon doing this, the girl from the citron did not die, and being so beautiful, the prince promised to marry her. He left her to go and get suitable clothes so she could accompany him to the palace, and there they would get married. As he was taking some time to return, the girl looked through the bushes where she was hiding, and saw a Negress coming to fill a pitcher with water. This woman, seeing the beautiful face reflected in the water, thought it was herself, and broke the pitcher, saying: "Such a lovely face carrying water! This cannot be!"

The girl couldn't refrain from laughing; the Negress looked around and found her, and extremely angry, pretended to be gentle and called the girl to come to her. When the girl was beside her, she stroked her hair and started to pick among the locks. Taking advantage of her distraction, the Negress stuck a pin into her ear, and the girl was turned into a dove. The prince, upon arriving and finding an ugly and dirty-looking negress in place of the lovely girl he had left, asked in surprise: "What became of the girl I left here?" "I am she," said the woman. "The sun toasted me while I was waiting for you."

The prince gave her the clothes he had brought and took her to the palace, where everyone was appalled at his choice. He wanted to fulfill his promise, and kept his shame to himself. The

---

[83] C. Pedroso, Contos *Populares Portugueses*, 47-52.

gardener, when watering the flowers, saw a white dove in the gardens, which asked:

> "*Gardener of the gardens, how are the king*
> *And his Black Maria doing?*"
> Surprised, the gardener answered:
> "*They feast and drink, and lead a splendid life.*
> *And the poor little dove is lost here!*"

The gardener went to tell the prince about the dove, and he marveled, saying: "Make a ribbon snare for it." The next day, the dove came again and asked the same question; the gardener answered similarly, and the dove flew off, saying: "A royal dove shall never fall prey to a ribbon snare."

The gardener went back to the prince with the news, and the prince said: "Set up a silver snare." This was done, but the dove flew away, saying: "A royal dove shall not fall prey to a silver snare."

When the gardener told the prince of the occurred, he said: "Now make a gold noose for it." The dove was captured, and when the prince, feeling quite sad, came to walk in his gardens, found it and started to stroke its head. He discovered the pin in the ear of the dove, and pulled it out. Right away, the girl he had left by the water reappeared, and he asked why she had suffered that fate. Hearing how the Negress came to the fountain, broke the pitcher, and then stroked her hair until she stuck the pin into her ear, the prince took her to the palace as his wife. Then, before the whole court, he asked her what should be done about the Black Maria. The maiden said: "I want a drum made out of her skin, so I can play it when I go out in the street; from her bones, I want a ladder to go down to the gardens."

Better done than said, and the royal couple lived happily from then on.

Synopsis 6: The White Little Dove and The Crooked Mooress[84]

Once upon a time, a young man went visiting his godmother who was the Queen of the Fairies. When he left her place, she gave him three quinces, telling him to cut open the fruits only when near to a water source. But he didn't enjoy the gift, for this fruit cannot be sucked, since its juice is sour. Then, disobeying his godmother, he decided to open one of the quinces, from where a beautiful lady emerged asking for some water. Since there was no water nearby, she fainted and died.

Walking a little bit further, he again decided to cut open the second quince, and an even more gracious damsel sprung up from the fruit. Again, this one couldn't survive either. Finally, he cut the third quince close to a stream of water and, this time, the young girl, who was the prettiest among the three, survived for he was able to quench her thirst. But since she was naked, the young man asked her to climb up on tree while he would fetch her some proper clothing.

Soon, a crooked Mooress approached to fetch some water for her mistress. When she bent over the water, she saw the damsel's image reflected and thought it was hers. Now sure that she was pretty enough to be married to a prince, instead of performing this fetching water business, she threw the jar against the rocks and broke it. The young lady up there in the tree couldn't help laughing. The crooked Mooress overheard it and then realized that the reflected image was not hers, but the damsel's. She then convinced the girl to climb down the tree and started caring for her hair. She then pricked a pin on the top of the girl's head. The beautiful young girl was then transformed into a white dove, and flew away.

When the young man came back, the crooked Mooress made him believe that she was the lady whom he had left there waiting for him. The ugliness he now saw she explained was caused by the sun, dust, heat and tiredness which overcame her during his

---

[84] R. Guimarães, *Lendas e Fábulas do Brasil*.

absence. And since he was a man of his word, he took this witch home and took good care of her.

But the young gentleman noticed that every day a little white dove would come by the branches of the tree, gazing curiously towards him. The crooked Mooress then became suspicious and wished to eat that gracious bird. No matter how much the young man tried to dissuade her from such a cruelty, she ended up convincing him, and he promised to catch it in a snare the next morning.

He prepared a snare made out of twine, but the little dove, touching it with her beak, said she would only be caught by a snare made of silver. And she flew away. The young man was impressed by the fact that the little white dove could even speak! In another day, he brought in the silver trap, but, again, the little dove refused it, saying that she would only step on a snare made out of gold. Then, a snare of gold was made, but once more she rejected it, for she would only accept a snare made of diamond. So, this time she allowed herself to be ensnared by the diamond noose. The crooked Mooress wanted to kill her at once, but the young man pondered and was fascinated by the many conditions imposed by the little dove. And while he admired and spoke to the little dove, he ran his hand over her head and found the pin. He took it out and, instantaneously, there it transformed into the beautiful damsel he had left waiting for him by the river.

The crooked Mooress wanted to flee, but they put her inside a barrel full of opened razors and made it roll down the hill. She died, and the young man and the damsel got married, had many children, and lived happy for many, many years.

REFERENCES

Abt, Theodor. *Introduction to Picture Interpretation According to C.G. Jung*. Einsiedeln, Switzerland: Daimon Verlag, 2005.

Aigle. http://www.theoi.com/Ouranios/AsklepiasAigle.html.

Alinei, Mario & Benozzo, Francesco. "Origini del megalitismo europeo: un approccio archeo-etno-dialettologico." Quaderni di Semantica, 2008.

de Barreira, Isidoro. "Tratado das significaçoens das plantas, flores, e fruttos, que se referem na Sagrada Escrittura : tiradas de divinas, e humanas letras, com suas breves considerações." http://objdigital.bn.br/acervo_digital/div_obrasraras/or_21_4_17/or_21_4_17_item1/index.html.

Basile, Giambattista. *Project Gutenberg's Stories from Pentamerone*. London: Macmillan and Co., Limited, 1911.

Berczi, Szaniszlo & Sano, Osamu & Takaki, Ryuji. "Snake Patterns in Eurasia/Japan and Their Implications." Forma. 16. 279, 2001.

Calvino, Italo. *Italian Folktales Selected and Retold*. New York: Pantheon Book, 1980.

Campbell, Joseph. *The Mysteries, Papers from the Eranos Yearbooks, Volume 2*. Princeton, NJ: Princeton University Press, 1978.

Chevalier, Jean & Gheerbrant, Alain. *Dictionary of Symbols*. London: Penguin, 1994.

Cirlot, Juan Eduardo. *A Dictionary of Symbols, Second Edition*. Milton Park, Oxfordshire: Taylor & Francis eLibrary, 2001.

Crane, Thomas Frederick. *The Love of the Three Oranges*. Cambridge, MA: The Riverside Press, 1885.

_____. *Italian Popular Tales*. Oxford: Oxford University Press, 2003.

David-Fierz, Linda & Hottinger, Mary. *The Dream of Poliphilo*. New York: Spring Publications, 1987.

Delahoyde, Michael. http://public.wsu.edu/~delahoyd/shakespeare/r&j2.html, 2012.

Edinger, Edward. *Ego and Archetype*. Boulder, CO: Shambhala, 1992.

Eliade, Mircea. *Shamanism: Archaic Techniques of Ecstasy*. Princeton, NJ: Princeton University Press, 1972.

von Franz, Marie-Louise. *Puer Aeternus: A Psychological Study of the Adult Struggle with the Paradise of Childhood*. Boston, MA: Sigo Press, 1970.

_____. *Individuation in Fairytales*. New York: Spring Publications, 1977.

_____. *The Passion of Perpetua: A Psychological Interpretation of Her Visions*. New York: Spring Publications, 1980.

_____. *The interpretation of Fairytales*. Boulder, CO: Shambhala, 1996.

_____. *Archetypal Patterns in Fairytales*. Toronto, Ontario: Inner City Books, 1997.

_____. *Dreams – A Study of the Dreams of Jung, Descartes, Socrates, and Other Historical Figures*. Boulder, CO: Shambhala, 1998.

_____. *Animus and Anima in Fairytales*. Toronto, Ontario: Inner City Books, 2002.

_____. *Interprétation du conte d'Apulée : L'âne d'or*. Fontaine Pierre, 2008.

Frazer, James George. *The Golden Bough*. London: Forgotten Books, 2008.

Gallop, Rodney. *Portugal - A Book of Folk Ways*. Cambridge: University Press, 1936.

Grazer, Brian, and Charles Fishman. *A Curious Mind: The Secret to a Bigger Life*. New York: Simon & Schuster, 2015.

Guimarães, Ruth. *Lendas e Fabulas do Brasil*. Taubaté: Livraria Selvagem, 2019.

Hannah, B. *The Inner Journey: Lectures and Essays on Jungian Psychology*. Ontario: Inner City Books, 2000.

Jung, Carl. *Psychology and Religion: West and East*. Princeton, NJ: Princeton University Press, 1966a.

_____. *Two Essays on Analytical Psychology*. Princeton, NJ: Princeton University Press, 1966b.

_____. *Mysterium Coniunctionis*. Princeton, NJ: Princeton University Press, 1970.

_____. *Alchemical Studies*. Princeton, NJ: Princeton University Press, 1983.

_____. *Man and His Symbols*. New York: Anchor Press, 1988.

_____. *Memories, Dreams, Reflections*. New York: Vintage Books, 1989a.

_____. *Analytical Psychology – Notes on the seminar given in 1925*. Princeton, NJ: Princeton University Press, 1989b.

_____. *Symbols of Transformation*. Princeton, NJ: Princeton University Press, 1990.

_____. *Jung Speaking: Interviews and Encounters*. Princeton, NJ: Princeton University Press, 1993.

_____. *Visions: Notes of the seminar given in 1930-1934 (Vol. I, II)*. Princeton, NJ: Princeton University Press, 1997.

_____. *The Red Book: Liber Novus* (S. Shamdasani, Ed.). New York: W.W. Norton & Company, 2009.

Kawan, Christine Shojaei. "Reflections of International Narrative Research on the example of the tale of the Three Oranges. http://www.folklore.ee/folklore/vol27/kawan.pdf.

Lindsay, Jack. *The Origins of Alchemy in Graeco-Roman Egypt.* New York: Frederick Muller, 1970.

Lispector, Clarice. *Perto do Coracao Selvagem*. Rio de Janeiro: Francisco Alves, 1990.

Machado, José Barbosa. "Análise Informáticolinguística de Três Versões do conto As Três Cidras do Amor," http://alfarrabio.di.uminho.pt/vercial/zips/machad17.pdf.

Magalhaes, J.V.C. *O Selvagem*. Livraria Itatiaia Editora. Colecao Reconquista do Brasil Vol. 16, 1975.

Maguire, Anne. *Skin Disease – A Message from the Soul: A Treatise from a Jungian Perspective of Psychosomatic Dermatology.* London: Free Association Books, 2004.

Mariani, John F. *The Dictionary of American Food and Drink.* New York: Hearst Books, 1994.

Mayer, Fanny Hagin & Kunio, Yanagita. Japanese Folk Tales. *Folklore Studies,* 11(1), i–97. https://doi.org/10.2307/1177324, 1952.

Onians, R.B. *The Origins of European Thought. Cambridge:* University Press, 1952.

Otto, Walter F. "The Meaning of the Eleusinian Mysteries" in *The Mysteries – Papers from the Eranos Yearbook*s. Princeton, NJ: Princeton University Press, 1990.

Pedroso, Consiglieri. *Contos Populares Portugueses*. Sao Paulo: Landi, 2001.

Pereira, Nunes. *Os indios Maues.* Rio [de Janeiro] Organização Simões, 1954.

Ratnasinghe, A. (2004). http://www.angelfire.com/planet/heritagesl2/nawagamuwa/nawagamuwa2.htm.

Romero, Silvio. *Contos Populares do Brasil.* Saõ Paulo, Brasil: Landy Editora, 2000.

Salapata, Gina. "The Tippling Serpent in the Art of Lakonia and Beyond." Hesperia: The Journal of the American School of Classical Studies at Athens 75, no. 4, 2006. https://www.jstor.org/stable/i25067997.

Smith, Zadie. *Swing Time*. New York: Penguin Press, 2016.

Stokes, Maive. *Indian Fairy Tales.* London: Ellis & White, 1880.

Ulanov, Ann & Ulanov, Barry. *Transforming Sexuality - The Archetypal World of Anima and Animus.* Boulder, CO: Shambhala, 1994.

Wilbert Johannes. *Puertas del Averno.* Sociedad de Ciencias Naturales la Salle.